W9-CBV-703

BROADWAY PRESENTS

Teens' Musical Theatre Anthology

FEMALE EDITION

A TREASURY OF SONGS FROM STAGE & FILM, SPECIALLY DESIGNED FOR TEEN SINGERS!

Includes Story Synopsis, Song Set-up, Audition Tips & 16-Bar Cut Suggestions

Edited & Compiled by **Lisa DeSpain**

Alfred Publishing Co., Inc.
16320 Roscoe Blvd., Suite 100
P.O. Box 10003
Van Nuys, CA 91410-0003

alfred.com

Copyright © 2009 by Alfred Publishing Co., Inc.
All rights reserved. Printed in USA.

ISBN-10: 0-7390-5797-9
ISBN-13: 978-0-7390-5797-1

Contents

Introduction

Theatrical songs are a perfect choice for the teen voice,
both the developing singer and the experienced performer.

For the vocal student, musical theater songs provide a wide range of challenges to strengthen the voice; lyrical melodies with interesting intervallic relationships, surprising and beautiful harmonic and melodic note choices, complex and constantly changing rhythms along with a large variety of singing styles (ballad, up tempo, swing, pop) and vocal techniques (legit-head voice, belt, mix). Also, due to the storytelling nature of theater songs, attention to diction and clarity of the lyrics is essential. In mastering the challenges of the musical theater repertoire, a singer will master all the techniques needed to create a superb instrument out of their voice.

Additionally, the art of performing a theater song lies in the combination of superb musicianship with a commitment to the drama, the story, the character, and emotional situation. I highly encourage working with a vocal teacher to master the vocal techniques needed and an acting coach to learn to act the song. Both are needed to deliver a successful performance or audition.

The repertoire included in this anthology will provide the teen singer with a comprehensive collection suitable for any theatrical audition. The music ranges from Broadway's Golden Age through today's differing pop, rock and contemporary musical theater styles. The collection is also balanced with a variety of ballad, medium and up tempo selections along with comedy and dramatic songs. Each piece was chosen specifically for its young female teen character and ingénue dramatic situation. The teen singer should feel confident walking into an audition situation singing any song from this collection, assured that the music will showcase her appropriately.

If utilizing this music for audition purposes, here are a few extra hints for success:

1. Choose a song in a similar style to the show you are auditioning for. Determine the year the show premiered and choose a song from around the same time period. Another excellent idea is to choose a song by the same composer but from a different show he/she has written.

2. Present a song in a similar style to the character you are auditioning for. Familiarize yourself with the musical style of your character. If it is a comedic role, sing a comedic song. If the character sings mostly ballads or dramatic material, present a dramatic ballad. You want the director to see you as the character. Remember to dress appropriately but not in costume.

3. Be prepared to sing a contrasting song. If you present an up tempo song first, have a good ballad ready just in case they ask for more and vice versa.

4. Always greet your accompanist in a friendly manner and discuss your needs for the audition. Clearly state the title of the song you will be singing and describe the style if your accompanist does not immediately recognize the song. Be sure to ask for your first pitch or the opening chord to get your ears oriented to the piano. Always thank your accompanist before you leave.

5. Be professional, courteous, efficient and confident. Remember, the people casting you want to see you succeed, so have fun!

—Lisa DeSpain

Lisa DeSpain is a New York City based musical theater director/composer and audition accompanist. She serves on faculty at Professional Performing Arts School, New York City's premiere public school for teens training for and performing on Broadway.

Notes Regarding 16-Bar Audition Cuts

The suggested cuts are intended to give the singer a polished, well-crafted audition, showcasing his/her musical, vocal, and acting skills in as succinct a time as possible.

Casting agents and directors are more interested in a well-crafted performance than policing the 16 measures. As such, the "16-bar " cuts may not be exactly 16-bars but will be completely appropriate for an audition situation. Bar numbers are indicated as m. #, e. g. bar 16 is indicated as m. 16.

110 in the Shade

The Show

Setting: A western state from dawn to midnight on a summer day in a time of drought

Lizzie Currie has one simple dream, to marry and have a family of her own. Lizzie believes she has been unsuccessful because she is plain and honest-spoken. The local sheriff, File briefly tries to court Lizzie, but the attempt ends badly due to File's pride and Lizzie's insecurity. A man named Starbuck arrives, claiming he has magical powers to make rain for a "small price." Lizzie confronts Starbuck on his con. Starbuck challenges Lizzie regarding her beliefs about herself. She begins to bloom under his attention and affection. Starbuck then attempts to replace Lizzie's simple dreams with more adventurous ones, hoping she will join him as a wanderer on the road. File soon gets word of a con man working the local towns and goes looking for Starbuck. When he sees Lizzie and Starbuck together, File realizes his true feelings for Lizzie. He drops his pride and openly professes his love. Instead of the dry life ahead, Lizzie is rained on with happiness and choices.

The Authors

Book by N. Richard Nash
Music by Harvey Schmidt
Lyrics by Tom Jones

New York Run

October 24, 1963 – August 9, 1964,
Broadhurst Theatre

The Songs

"Raunchy"

Lizzie has been watching the local girls flirt with the men at the town picnic. She jokes with her father about all the things she might try in order to attract the mens' attention.

Song type
Standard, Golden Age, Medium Tempo, Comedy (Belt)

Suggested 16-bar Audition Cut
m. 17, beat 2 through end of m. 31, then cut to m. 76 and sing to the end.

Have the accompanist give a bell tone starting pitch "E." Sing in measure 17, starting on beat 2, *"I'll be so…"* a cappella and freely. At the downbeat of measure 18, begin singing in tempo. Sing through measure 31, *"every night. I'm a…"* then cut to measure 76 singing, *"raunchy kind of gal."* Sing to the end.

"Is It Really Me"

For the first time, Lizzie experiences romantic affection in the arms of Starbuck. She is awed by the power of love and how it has helped her to recognize that she is truly beautiful.

Song type
Standard, Golden Age, Ballad, Dramatic (Legit)

Suggested 16-bar Audition Cut
m. 22 through end of m. 37, then cut to m. 40 for the final chord.

Have the accompanist play measure 22 as an introduction and then repeat the measure. Enter singing on the repeat, *"Now here I am…"* Sing through measure 37. Skip over measures 38 and 39, going directly to measure 40 for the final chord.

25th Annual Putnam County Spelling Bee

The Show

Setting: a middle school gymnasium, the present

At the 25th Annual Putnam County Spelling Bee, emotions and expectations are high. As the competition unfolds, each speller learns valuable lessons. Chip Tolentino would like to repeat his first place win from last year but falters, distracted by a pretty girl in the audience. Leaf Connybear thinks he's "not that smart" but soon realizes that he is. Marcy Park, who has been pushed to excel beyond perfection, finds the joy in just being normal. Logainne Schwarzandsrubeniere grapples with her ideologies of right and wrong. In the end, the competition between William Barfee and Olive Ostrovsky becomes a celebration of their competence and joy in their new-found friendship. William learns to think of someone else first and Olive finds love and friendship from others to help heal the void of absent parents.

The Authors

Book by Rachel Sheinkin
Music and lyrics by William Finn

New York Run

May 2, 2005 – January 20, 2008, Circle in the Square Theatre

The Song

"I Speak Six Languages"

Marcy Park sings her list of brilliant accomplishments, but with some anger and resentment. She eventually realizes the joy in just being normal, and purposely misspells to take herself out of the competition.

Song type

Contemporary, Up Tempo, Comedy (Belt)

Suggested 16-bar Audition Cut

m. 53 through the end of m. 64, then cut to m. 95 and sing to the end.

Have accompanist vamp on measure 53 for the introduction. Enter singing *"I achieve my goals."* Sing through measure 64, *"I get no real enjoyment, but…"* At measure 95, <u>do not</u> sing the word *"class"* on beat 1. Instead, rest and then enter singing *"I speak six languages."* Sing to the end.

Camelot

The Show

Setting: In and around Camelot and a battlefield in France, a long time ago

Through a treaty, Guenevere and King Arthur are betrothed. Both are frightened by the idea of marriage to a stranger but fall in love when they meet and marry happily. King Arthur creates a civilization based on higher ideals, peace, justice, and brotherhood, known as the Knights of the Round Table. The renowned French knight, Lancelot du Lac arrives to join the order. King Arthur accepts him immediately but Guenevere is uneasy around Lancelot. Guenevere and Lancelot soon recognize their feelings of love for each other and struggle to suppress them because of their love for Arthur. Mordred, Arthur's illegitimate son, wishing the downfall of King Arthur and Camelot, lays a trap for Guevenere and Lancelot. When they meet in Guenevere's chambers to say goodbye, Mordred enters, accusing them of treason. Although Arthur forgives them, he is bound to punish them according the laws of Camelot. Lancelot rescues Guenevere from her death sentence but Arthur must now follow him to France for war. Arthur takes comfort in the presence of a young boy who has followed Arthur to the battlefield intent on joining Arthur's Camelot and its ideals.

The Authors

Book by Alan Jay Lerner
Music by Frederick Loewe
Lyrics by Alan Jay Lerner
Based on the T. H. White novel, "The Once and Future King."

New York Run

December 3, 1960 – January 5, 1963, Majestic Theatre

The Song

"Simple Joys of Maidenhood"

Guinevere, arriving in Camelot, escapes her carriage. In hiding, she bemoans her fate of being wedded to a total stranger at such a young age, having never experienced the joys of being young and in love.

Song type

Standard, Golden Age, Medium Tempo (Legit)

Suggested 16-bar Audition Cut

m. 45 through the end of m. 56, then cut to m. 61 and sing to the end.

Have the accompanist give a bell tone starting pitch "F." Enter singing in tempo, *"Where are the simple joys…"* Sing through measure 56, *"…kin for me? Oh,"* then cut to the beginning of measure 61 singing, *"… where are the simple joys?"* Sing to the end.

Chicago

The Show

Setting: Chicago, Illinois, late 1920s

Roxie Hart has shot her lover in a cold-blooded murder. Imprisoned and awaiting trial, she meets the infamous double murderess, Velma Kelly, who has been using her publicity to further her stage career. Roxie also has dreams of a stage career and begins to play at Velma's game, starting with hiring Velma's lawyer, the slick Billy Flynn. Flynn creates a dramatic and dazzling case of self-defense for Roxie, which bumps Velma off the front page. When another female inmate is hung for murder, Roxie and Velma realize it could be the end for them. Billy wraps up their trials quickly, using some "razzle dazzle" to have them found innocent. The minute Roxie's trial ends, another sensationalistic murder takes place, stealing all her publicity. Velma and Roxie realize that if they work together, they can salvage their careers in a sister-act.

The Authors

Book by Fred Ebb and Bob Fosse
Music by John Kander
Lyrics by Fred Ebb
Based on the play *"Chicago"*
by Maurine Dallas Watkins.

New York Run

June 3, 1975 – August 27, 1975, 46th Street Theatre

The Song

"Roxie"

Roxie realizes that this murder thing might not be so bad after all. If she plays her cards right, she just might be able to use the publicity to launch her vaudeville career.

Song type
Standard, Medium Swing, Comedy

Suggested 16-bar Audition Cut
m. 57 through m. 73, beat 1.

Have the accompanist play measures 57-58 for an introduction. Enter singing at measure 59, *"From just some dumb…"* End on beat 1 of measure 73, singing *"…Hart!"* If desired, add the optional spoken line, *"Thank you."* (see m.115).

Damn Yankees

The Show

Setting: Washington D.C., sometime in the future

Joe Boyd is passionate about his baseball team, the Washington Senators, who are losing the pennant race. The mysterious Applegate appears and offers Joe the chance to help his team…for the price of his soul. Joe accepts but insists on an escape clause, intent on returning to his wife, Meg, whom he loves. Joe becomes an instant celebrity star player and the Washington Senators become a winning team. Applegate sends out his best home-wrecker, Lola, to tempt Joe into forgetting about Meg. When Lola is unsuccessful, Applegate starts a rumor that Joe is really Shifty McCoy, a baseball player in hiding, known for "throwing" the game. While defending his honor in a court, Joe misses the deadline for his escape clause and loses his soul to Applegate. Joe then learns that Applegate is really a fan of the Yankees and plans to throw the final pennant game to them. During a fly ball to Joe's outfield, he changes Joe back into an old man hoping he'll miss. Despite Applegate's revenge, Joe catches the fly ball, the Senators win the pennant, and Joe keeps running all the way home to Meg.

The Authors

Book by George Abbott and Douglass Wallop
Music and Lyrics by Richard Adler and Jerry Ross
Based on the novel, *The Year the Yankees Lost the Pennant* by Douglass Wallop.

New York Run

May 5, 1955 – October 12, 1957, 46th Street Theatre

The Song

"A Little Brains, A Little Talent"

Lola has been given the task of corrupting Joe. She sings about her past conquests and her special skills in getting the job done.

Song type
Standard, Golden Age, Medium Tempo, Comedy

Suggested 16-bar Audition Cut
m. 98, beat 3, through the end of m. 116, then cut to m. 119 and sing to the end.

Have the accompanist give a bell tone starting pitch "A." Begin the piano introduction on measure 98 beat 3, in tempo. Enter singing in measure 99, *"Bring on that boy…"* Sing through the end of measure 116, *"on the…"* Cut to the beginning of measure 119, singing the lyric *"…latter"* thereby completing the phrase. Sing to the end.

The Fantasticks

The Show

Setting: a backyard, the present

Luisa and Matt are young, dreaming of adventure, and ardently in love, yet separated by a backyard wall. Their fathers have created a feud, using reverse psychology with the real intent being for their children to fall in love. For the finishing touches, they hire a bandit, El Gallo, to abduct Luisa. During a romantic interlude between Luisa and Matt, El Gallo stages his elaborate "abduction" ending with victory for Matt and a sealed romance. Yet love and friendship change in the second act. The lovers break up, Matt leaves to adventure around the world and the fathers rebuild the wall and actually feud. El Gallo returns, romances Luisa, and then abandons her with a broken heart. Matt returns from his adventures, disillusioned by the world. As both the fathers and the lovers mend their relationships, they find deeper understanding to the complex world of the heart.

The Authors

Book and Lyrics by Tom Jones
Music by Harvey Schmidt

New York Run

May 3, 1960 – January 13, 2002, The Sullivan Street Playhouse (Off-Broadway)

The world's longest running musical, 17,162 performances.

The Song

"Much More"

Young Luisa has yet to experience the things of the world. She sings, perhaps naively, of her dreams and the adventures she wishes to take with her life.

Song type

Standard, Medium Tempo, Dramatic (Legit)

Suggested 16-bar Audition Cut

m. 41, beat 4, to the end.

Have the accompanist give a bell tone starting pitch "F." Enter singing in tempo, *"to do the things I've dreamed about…"* Sing to the end.

Finian's Rainbow

The Show

Setting: Rainbow Valley, Missitucky, USA, late 1940s

Finian and his daughter, Sharon, arrive in Rainbow Valley with a magical pot of gold, which Finian has stolen from the leprechaun, Og. Finian believes burying gold in the ground around Fort Knox will cause it to multiply. They meet Woody and his mute sister, Susan, who are about to lose their land to the racist Senator Rawkins. Finian pays the back taxes and is granted rights to a small portion of the land. Woody and Sharon fall in love. Og arrives wanting his gold back. Without his gold, Og is turning mortal. Confused by his human emotions, when he sees Sharon, he falls in love. Sharon sees Rawkins mistreating a Negro sharecropper and wishes that Rawkins knew what it felt like to be black. Sharon is unknowingly standing over the magical pot of gold and therefore, her wish comes true. She is charged with witchcraft. Meanwhile, Og meets Susan and falls in love…again. He wishes Susan could speak and tell him where to find his gold. The wish is granted as he is sitting atop the hidden pot of gold. With one wish left, he spends it to help Sharon. Og is now forever destined to be mortal, which is not so bad because he has Susan.

The Authors

Book by E.Y. Harburg and Fred Saidy
Music by Burton Lane
Lyrics by E.Y. Harburg

New York Run

January 10, 1947 – October 2, 1948, 46th Street Theatre

The Song

"How Are Things in Glocca Morra"

Sharon is wondering why her father left Ireland in such a hurry. She wishes to go back and tempts Finian by remembering life in their home of Glocca Morra.

Song type

Standard, Golden Age, Ballad (Legit)

Suggested 16-bar Audition Cut

m. 18 to the end.

Have accompanist give a bell tone starting pitch "A-flat." Enter singing, *"How are things in…"* Sing to the end.

Funny Girl

The Show

Setting: New York, Baltimore, Long Island and in various theaters shortly before and after World War I

Nothing will stop Fanny Brice from getting into show business. Although she is not beautiful like the showgirls, she has the talent to be funny. She becomes a famous comedic star with the Ziegfeld Follies. She meets the charming entrepreneur, Nick Arnstein, who falls for Fanny, as she is different from all the other girls. Fanny also falls for Nick. When he promises to return to Fanny after a deal in Monte Carlo, Fanny refuses to listen and decides to do things her own way. She leaves the Follies and follows Nick to Europe. They return married. Fanny continues her successful theatrical career but Nick flounders to find equal footing in the marriage. Fanny insists on bankrolling his business ventures which fail, leaving Nick emasculated. In a desperate attempt to make his own money, Nick participates in a fraud scam and is arrested. Fanny begins to understand that she has driven Nick to this action by loving him too much. When Nick finally returns to her, he confesses that they must part. Fanny pretends to support his decision; after all she is one of the greatest actresses on stage.

The Authors

Book by Isobel Lennart
Music by Jules Styne
Lyrics by Bob Merrill
Based on the real life of vaudeville star, Fanny Brice.

New York Run

March 26, 1964 – July 1, 1967, Winter Garden Theatre, Majestic Theatre, and Broadway Theatre

The Songs

"Don't Rain on My Parade"

Fanny Brice makes a rash decision to leave the Ziegfeld Follies and follow Nick Arnstein to Europe despite everyone's protest, including Nick's. She refuses to listen, insisting that her way is best.

Song type
Standard, Golden Age, Up Tempo, Dramatic (Belt)

Suggested 16-bar Audition Cut
m. 74 through end of m. 94, then cut to m. 101 for the final chord.

Have the accompanist play the chord on beat 1 in measure 74. Enter singing, *"I'll march my…"* Sing through measure 94, and then cut to the ending chord in measure 101. If the accompanist is unfamiliar with this song, be sure to talk through the tempo changes occurring at measures 75, 80, 91 and 93.

"The Music That Makes Me Dance"

Fanny eagerly awaits the arrival of Nick, who has been released from prison. As she prepares to go on stage, she realizes not only her mistakes that drove Nick to such extreme measures, but also how deeply she loves him.

Song type
Standard, Golden Age, Ballad, Dramatic

Suggested 16-bar Audition Cut
m. 39 to the end.

Have the accompanist give a bell tone starting pitch "A." Enter singing in tempo, *"In ev'ry way…"* Sing to the end.

An additional option would be to begin singing at the pick-up to measure 32, *"He'll sleep and he'll rise…"* singing to the end.

Hairspray

The Show

Setting: Baltimore, 1962

Tracy Turnblad is a slightly overweight yet happy-go-lucky and forward thinking teenager. She has one big dream, to dance on the "Corny Collins Show!" The mean-spirited and prejudicial Mrs. Von Tussle, the TV show's manager dismisses Tracy at an audition. Nevertheless, Tracy triumphs and is asked to join the show when Corny Collins sees her performing a dance step she learned from her "negro" friend, Seaweed. Her first day on the Corny Collins Show, she announces her wish that every day on the show was "Negro Day!" She gains the admiration of the show's heart-throb, Link Larkin. Having achieved her dream, Tracy inspires and empowers those around her. She helps her mother to be brave and accept herself now matter what her weight. She inspires her friends to find true friendships and romance despite racial differences. And she inspires the whole Baltimore community to tear down the prevailing racial boundaries, welcoming them into the '60s and beyond. And she gets the guy.

The Authors

Book by Mark O'Donnell and Thomas Meehan
Music by Marc Shaiman
Lyrics by Scott Whitman and Marc Shaiman
Based on the John Waters film *Hairspray*, by New Line Cinema.

New York Run

August 15, 2002 – January 4, 2009,
Neil Simon Theatre

Film musical version of *Hairspray* released July 20, 2007

The Song

"A New Girl In Town"
(from the film musical)

Tracy is a sensation on the Corny Collins Show much to the chagrin of Amber Von Tussle, the show's reining diva. Amber sings a not so subtle "new pop hit" reflecting her true feelings towards Tracy. Of course, on "Negro Day" the trio, "The Dynamites," also sing the hit with a lot more panache!

Song type

Contemporary, Up Tempo, 60's Pop, Comedic

Suggested 16-bar Audition Cut

Option 1

m. 6 through the end of m. 17, then cut to m. 30 through the end of m. 38.

Have the accompanist play measure 6 as an introduction. Enter singing at the end of the measure, *"The…"* Have accompanist play through measure 17, and then cut to measure 30. Sing the bridge *"She's hip. So cool."* At measure 39 beat 1, have the accompanist play "A flat" octaves instead of the written "A" for an ending.

Option 2

m. 40 through the end of m. 53, then cut to m. 68 and sing to the end.

Have the accompanist give a bell tone starting pitch "D." Enter singing the pick-up in measure 40 in tempo, *"The new girl in town…."* Sing through measure 52 in tempo *"We'd like to say…"* At measure 53 sing, *"to the new girl in…"* freely. (See m. 67.) Cut to measure 68 singing, *"town"* thereby completing the phrase. Have the accompanist play measure 69 for a "button" finish.

Kiss Me Kate

The Show

Setting: Ford's Theater, Baltimore, Maryland, June 1948

Fred Graham is staging a musical version of *The Taming of the Shrew*. To boost box-office sales, he casts his ex-wife, now Hollywood movie star, Lilli Vanessi in the leading role. But Mr. Graham has a flirtatious eye on his co-star Lois Lane. Lois returns the flirtation much to the chagrin of her sweetheart, Bill Calhoun. Fred and Lilli begin the evening by fighting but also realize they still have romantic feelings for each other. Meanwhile, Bill Calhoun has signed a $10,000 I.O.U. for a gambling debt using Fred Graham's name. Fred sends a bouquet of flowers with a love note to Lois, which is mistakenly delivered to Lilli. Touched by Fred's romantic gesture, Lilli slips the card, yet unread, into her costume near her heart. During an offstage moment, Lilli reads the card. Scorned, she returns to the stage. Using their roles of the feuding couple, Kathryn and Petruchio, Fred and Lilli engage in a full-scale on-stage battle. At intermission Lilli threatens to walk off the production. Meanwhile, two thugs have come to collect on the gambling I.O.U. To keep Lilli from walking out, Fred convinces the gangsters that if the show runs, he can pay the debt. They dress in Shakespearian costumes and follow Lilli for the rest of the production. In the end, Fred and Lilli recognize they still love each other and are reconciled.

The Authors

Book by Bella Spewack
Music and Lyrics by Cole Porter
Based on William Shakespeare's *Taming of the Shrew.*

New York Run

December 30, 1948 – July 29, 1951, New Century Theatre and Shubert Theatre

The Song

"Always True To You In My Fashion"

Lois flirts with every man, which troubles her sweetheart, Bill. He questions whether she cares for him at all. She explains that although she may flirt with many men, Bill is the one man she is true to "in her own fashion."

Song type

Standard, Golden Age, Up Tempo, Comedy

Suggested 16-bar Audition Cut

m. 48 through the end of m. 60, then cut to the 2nd ending (m. 66), and sing to the end.

Have the accompanist play measures 48-49 for an introduction. Enter singing on beat 4 of measure 49, *"There's a madman known as Mack…"* Skip the first ending (measures 61-65) and go to the second ending (measure 66). Sing to the end.

The Little Mermaid

The Show

Setting: The sea and Kingdom of Prince Eric, the present

Ariel is the youngest mermaid princess, daughter of King Triton. She is fascinated by the human world and wonders what life would be like up above. One day, while watching humans aboard a sailing ship, she sees a young prince. When a storm causes the ship to sink, she rescues the young prince from drowning. Ariel realizes she has fallen in love and makes a deal with the sea witch, Ursula, trading her beautiful voice for a pair of legs. Unfortunately, part of the deal stipulates that the prince must fall in love with Ariel within three days. If he does not, Ariel will forever be in the clutches of the terrible sea witch. After much sorcery, courage, and sacrifice, true love wins the day.

The Authors

Book by Doug Wright
Music by Alan Menken
Lyrics by Howard Ashman and Glenn Slater
Based on the Hans Christian Anderson fairy tale "The Little Mermaid" and the 1998 animated Disney movie, *The Little Mermaid*.

New York Run

January 10, 2008 – Present, Lunt-Fontanne Theatre

The Song

"Part of Your World"

Ariel has collected many interesting artifacts from the human world and keeps them hidden in a secret treasure trove. As she admires her collection, she dreams of all the wonderful things she could see and experience in the human world above her watery realm.

Song type

Contemporary Ballad, Dramatic, Disney

Suggested 16-bar Audition Cut

m. 70 through the end of m. 91, then cut to m. 96 for the final chord.

Have accompanist begin at measure 70 for the introduction. Enter singing at pick up in measure 70 *"And ready to know..."* At the end of measure 91, have the accompanist cut to the final chord in measure 96.

Little Shop Of Horrors

The Show

Setting: Skid Row in a decade not too long before our own

Seymour Krelborn is the lowly and browbeaten assistant at Mr. Mushnik's Plant Shop, a customer-forsaken florist on Skid Row. He is in love with Audrey, the other assistant but is too timid to express his feelings. Audrey also has self-esteem issues as she is dating a sadistic dentist who beats and demeans her. One day Mushnik announces that he must close because business is bad. Audrey insists that if Seymour could display this very odd plant he has been nurturing, it will attract customers. Within seconds of displaying Audrey II (named after Audrey) in the window, a customer enters and purchases all the roses left in the shop. Mushnik's is back in business and Audrey II becomes an overnight sensation. But keeping Audrey II alive is fraught with difficulty. Audrey II only thrives when she is fed blood. When Seymour has practically drained his own veins, Audrey II tempts Seymour to feed him a whole person. Aghast, Seymour cannot imagine the horror of killing a person...that is until he sees Orin, the dentist, beat Audrey. Soon bodies are suspiciously disappearing until the only thing left at Mushnik's is Audrey II.

The Authors

Book and Lyrics by Howard Ashman
Music by Alan Menken

New York Run

July 27, 1982 – November 1, 1987, Orpheum Theater (Off-Broadway)

The Song

"Somewhere That's Green"

The girls of Skid Row suggest Audrey dump her sadistic boyfriend for Seymour. Audrey believes Seymour could never love a girl "with a past." However, she does harbor a small dream of their future together.

Song type

Contemporary Ballad, Comedic (Belt/Mix)

Suggested 16-bar Audition Cut

m. 58, beat 4, to the end.

Have the accompanist give a bell tone starting pitch "B." Enter singing *"I'm his December bride..."* Sing to the end.

Little Women

The Show

Setting: Concord, Massachusetts, and New York City, Christmas 1863 – spring 1867

Jo March loves her sisters. Together the sisters make a pact to remain together forever. However, that pact is short-lived as Meg, the oldest daughter soon finds love and marries. Jo's best friend is Laurie, the boy next door. Although Laurie knows of Jo's desire to become a writer, he eventually confesses his love for Jo and asks for her hand in marriage. Jo feels betrayed. She leaves for New York City to follow her dream. In New York she befriends the German Professor Baher who is not impressed with Jo's sensationalistic writing, believing her capable of much more. Jo returns to Concord when she learns that her younger sister, Beth, is gravely ill. Beth passes away, but not without encouraging Jo to continue following her dreams. Jo soon realizes how to keep Beth's memory alive. She begins writing the stories of her sisters. She sends the manuscript to Professor Baher. He arrives in Concord not only with the good news that the manuscript will be published, but also to tell her of his admiration for her writing and to confess his feelings for Jo.

The Authors

Book by Allan Knee
Music by Jason Howland
Lyrics by Mindi Dickstein
Based on the classic novel, "Little Women," by Louise May Alcott.

New York Run

January 23, 2005 – May 22, 2005, Virginia Theatre

The Song

"Astonishing"

Jo feels betrayed. Laurie has broken his vow of friendship by proposing marriage. She wonders how she will find her way without her best friend. She promises herself she will not fail her dreams. She will be astonishing.

Song type
Contemporary, Medium Tempo, Dramatic (Belt)

Suggested 16-bar Audition Cut
m. 90 to the end.

Have the accompanist give a bell tone starting pitch "G." Enter singing in tempo *"I will blaze until I…."* Sing to the end.

Mamma Mia!

The Show

Setting: On a tiny Greek island, the present

Sophie is preparing to marry her sweetheart, Sky, and would like her father to walk her down the aisle. Problem is, she does not know who her father is. She secretly sends wedding invitations to the three loves of her mother's life. All three possible fathers arrive, which sends Donna, Sophie's mother, into hysterics. Sophie had thought it would be easy to tell who her father was, but cannot. She spends time with each man, hoping to recognize one as her father. As each story reveals itself, Sophie's ideals of love, marriage, fidelity, and family are challenged. In the end, Sophie realizes that although she loves Sky, she is not quite ready for marriage; while Donna reunites with and finally marries the man she loved most.

The Authors

Book by Catherine Johnson
Music and Lyrics by Benny Andersson and Björn Ulvaeus

New York Run

October 18, 2001 – present, Winter Garden Theatre

The Song

"Mamma Mia!"

Donna becomes hysterical when she walks into her taverna and finds all three of her former lovers waiting there. She flees into the arms of her best friends for comfort.

Song type
Contemporary, Up Tempo, '70s Pop, Comedy

Suggested 16-bar Audition Cut
m. 51 to the end.

Have the accompanist play measures 51–52 for an introduction. Enter singing at measure 53 *"Mamma Mia, here I go again."* Sing to the end.

A Man Of No Importance

The Show

Setting: Dublin, spring 1964

Alfie Byrne is a middle-aged bachelor with a passion for the works of Oscar Wilde. He works as a bus conductor where he entertains the passengers with poetry recitations. At night, he directs a community theater group dedicated to the works of Mr. Wilde. A new passenger arrives, a beautiful girl named Adele, whom Alfie believes is perfect to play the princess Salome in his next production. Alfie tries to recruit Robbie, the handsome young bus driver to play the leading man role, hoping to link Adele and Robbie. Robbie confesses to romantic interests elsewhere yet refuses to reveal her name. Alfie finally confesses to himself his feelings of love for Robbie. Confused by his feelings, Alfie attempts to follow his inclinations, but is lead into a trap and beaten. When Alfie's homosexual status becomes public, everyone abandons him, save Adele. Robbie then appears saying that although he cannot return that kind of love, Alfie is his friend. He would be honored to play the lead in Alfie's production of *Salome*.

The Authors

Book by Terrance McNally
Music by Stephen Flaherty
Lyrics by Lynn Ahrens

New York Run

September 12, 2002 – December 29, 2002, Lincoln Center, Mitzi E. Newhouse Theatre

The Song

"Princess"

Alfie asks Adele to play the role of the Princess Salome in his theatrical production. Adele replies that she is neither an actor nor a princess. Alfie sees more in her and this belief causes Adele to reflect on her limited belief in herself.

Song type
Contemporary, Medium Tempo, Dramatic (Mix)

Suggested 16-bar Audition Cut
m. 46 to the end.

Have accompanist vamp measure 46-47 for an introduction. At the repeat, enter singing *"I don't suppose I'll ever..."* Sing to the end.

Mary Poppins

The Show

Setting: London, 1910

Jane and Michael Banks are difficult children and running through nannies at an alarming rate. Magically, Mary Poppins appears at the Banks household. She uses magical powers to teach Jane and Michael important lessons. But the children are not the only ones in the Banks household in need of Mary Poppins' help. Their father, Mr. George Banks, is preoccupied with his work at the bank. Their mother, Winifred, is preoccupied with Mr. Banks' unhappiness. In the end, Mary Poppins helps everyone at the Banks household realize that their family is the most important thing of all.

The Authors

Book by Julian Fellowes
Music and lyrics by Richard M. Sherman and Robert B. Sherman
Based on a series of Mary Poppins novels written by P.L. Travers.

New York Run

November 16, 2005 – Present, New Amsterdam Theatre

The Song

"Practically Perfect"

Mary Poppins arrives at the Banks' household and promptly takes charge. She explains her distinct qualification and merit for the position.

Song type
Contemporary, Up Tempo, Comedic, Disney

Suggested 16-bar Audition Cut
m. 13 through m. 42, beat 1.

Have accompanist play measure 13 for the introduction. Enter singing *"I'm practically perfect..."* At measure 42, have the accompanist play a "C chord" for the ending instead of continuing on with the written notes.

My Fair Lady

The Show
Setting: London, 1912

Eliza Doolittle is a young flower seller on the streets of London where her cockney accent confines her to a lower social class. Henry Higgins, a professor of phonetics, records her accent one day in the market and then boasts of how he could change her manner of speech and pass her off as a lady. Eliza, wanting to better herself, presents herself at Professor Higgins's door the next day asking for lessons. At first the work is difficult and many battles ensue between Eliza and Professor Higgins, but Eliza eventually masters her speech and Professor Higgins passes her off to high society. Along the way, Freddy, a young blue blood, falls quite in love with Eliza. Higgins is boastfully proud of himself and vainly celebrates his accomplishments, completely ignoring Eliza's part in the success. When Eliza flees Professor Higgins' household in confusion and outrage, Higgins begins to acknowledge the true nature of his feelings for Eliza.

The Authors
Book and lyrics by Alan Jay Lerner
Music by Frederick Loewe
Based on the play *Pygmalion* by Bernard Shaw.

New York Run
March 15, 1956 – September 29, 1962, Hellinger Theatre, Broadhurst Theatre, and the Broadway Theatre

The Song

"Show Me"
Eliza flees Professor Higgins' home in a fit of rage and frustration after he fails to acknowledge her part in her successful society debut. He is also clueless as to her true feelings for him. As she flees the house, her ardent young suitor, Freddy, is waiting, once again professing his ardor. Angry that everyone talks but no one takes action, she sings.

Song type
Standard, Golden Age, Up Tempo, Dramatic

Suggested 16-bar Audition Cut
m. 47 through the end of m. 68, then cut to the 2nd ending (m. 73) and sing to the end.

Have accompanist vamp measure 47–48 for an introduction. When ready, enter singing, *"Haven't your lips longed for my touch…"* At the end of measure 68, skip to the second ending (m. 73) and sing to the end.

My One and Only

The Show
Setting: New York, a desert island, and Morocco, 1927

Captain Billy Buck Chandler dreams of nothing but becoming the first man to fly solo over the Atlantic Ocean…until he catches a glimpse of Edith Herbert, ex-channel swimmer and star in Prince Nicolai's International Aquacade. Yet all is not well at the Aquacade. Prince Nikki is blackmailing Edith, forcing her to stay with his show as his star attraction. Edith forgets her worries by attending the cinema and it is there where Billy finally "accidentally" meets Edith. They fall in love. Edith persuades Billy to fly her from the clutches of Prince Nikki to Cuba. They are sabotaged by Prince Nikki and land on a desert island. Their paradise is interrupted by Prince Nikki, and Edith returns to the show under threat that the Prince will reveal her past. With both lovers despondent, Edith runs away again and Billy goes searching for her in his airplane. He finds her in Morocco, the setting of the film they were watching when they first met. They return to America, marry and live happily ever after.

The Authors
Book by Peter Stone and Timothy S. Mayer
Music by George Gershwin
Lyrics by Ira Gershwin

New York Run
May 1, 1983 – March 3, 1985, St. James Theatre

The Song

"Boy Wanted"
Swimming star Edith Herbert tells of her dreams of falling in love, with a very clear list of her ideal sweetheart's qualifications.

Song type
Standard, Medium Tempo, Comedic

Suggested 16-bar Audition Cut
m. 43 through the end of m. 66, then cut to the 2nd ending (m. 69) and sing to the end.

Have accompanist play measures 43–44 for the introduction. Enter singing at measure 45, *"He must be tender and true."* At the end of measure 66, skip to the second ending (m. 69) and sing to the end. An additional option would be to sing the second verse, *"If he has oodles of charm."*

Once On This Island

The Show

Setting: An island in the French Antilles, the present

Ti Moune, a young peasant girl, lives on an island ruled by the gods and shared by two classes who can never meet, the peasants and the "grands hommes." One day, Ti Moune sees a handsome young man, Daniel, of the "grande homme" class and falls in love. She prays to the gods for a grander fate. The gods grant this wish to prove who is the more powerful, Erzulie, the goddess of love, or Papa Ge, the god of death. The rain god, Agwe, causes Daniel's car to crash, bringing him into Ti Moune's care. When Daniel is near death, Ti Moune makes a pact with Papa Ge, promising to give up her own life if Daniel is spared. Through her love, Daniel survives. He too loves Ti Moune but will not break with tradition and marry her. Papa Ge appears offering another bargain. If Ti Moune kills Daniel, she can live. Erzulie appears and reminds Ti Moune of her great capacity for love. Ti Moune refuses to kill Daniel. Love triumphs death. Although Ti Moune dies, she is resurrected as a beautiful tree whose spirit helps set the following generations free to love.

The Authors

Book and Lyrics by Lynn Ahrens
Music by Stephen Flaherty
Based on the story, My Love, My Love by Rosa Guy a Caribbean adaptation of the Little Mermaid fairy tale.

New York Run

October 18, 1990 – December 1, 1991, Booth Theatre

The Song

"Waiting for Life to Begin"

Ti Moune catches a glimpse of a handsome stranger and wonders if he is part of a grander fate for her. She sings her prayer to the gods.

Song type

Contemporary, Up Tempo, Dramatic (Belt)

Suggested 16-bar Audition Cut

m. 118, beat 4, to the end.

Have the accompanist give a bell tone starting pitch "D." Enter singing in tempo, *"You spared my life…"* Sing to the end.

Once Upon a Mattress

The Show

Setting: A small medieval kingdom, Spring, 1492

The overbearing Queen Aggravain sabotages every effort made by the many young princesses wishing to marry her son, Prince Dauntless. Unfortunately, there is a law stating that no one in the kingdom can marry until Prince Dauntless weds. The Honorable Sir Harry is determined to marry the lovely Lady Larken, therefore he sets off for faraway lands and returns with an unlikely candidate: Princess Winnifred from the swamps. It's love at first sight for Prince Dauntless and Winnifred, so the Queen sets about planning her most difficult challenge yet. She places a small pea under twenty mattresses to test Princess Winnifred's "sensitivity." The Queen does everything in her power to exhaust Princess Winnifred: dancing, spells, and sleeping draughts. Despite Queen Aggravain's efforts, Princess Winnifred passes the challenge with the help of some crafty courtiers and to the joy of everyone in the kingdom but the Queen.

The Authors

Book by Jay Thompson, Marshall Barer, and Dean Fuller
Music by Mary Rodgers
Lyrics by Marshall Barer
Based on the fairy tale, "The Princess and the Pea."

New York Run

May 11, 1959 – July 21, 1960, Phoenix Theatre, Alvin Theatre, Winter Garden Theatre, Cort Theatre, and St. James Theatre

The Song

"Shy"

Princess Winnifred has just swum the moat, impatient to meet the very shy Prince Dauntless. When she asks for the Prince, no one steps forward. She encourages him to make himself known, claiming that it is okay to be shy. After all, she is shy, too.

Song type

Standard, Golden Age, Up Tempo, Comedic (Belt)

Suggested 16-bar Audition Cut

m. 39 through the end of m. 57, then cut to the 2nd ending (m. 60) and sing to the end.

Have the accompanist give a bell tone starting pitch "F." Enter singing a cappella in tempo, *"I'm aware that it's wrong…"* At the end of measure 57, skip to the second ending (m. 60) and sing to the end.

Pajama Game

The Show

Setting: The Sleep-Tite Pajama Factory, Cedar Rapids, 1950s

A strike is imminent at the Sleep-Tite Pajama Factory where the Union workers are demanding a 7 ½ cent raise. The factory's new Superintendent, Sid, meets Babe, a Union organizer, and is smitten. At first Babe claims she is not interested but eventually falls in love. However, when Babe stages a slow-down at the factory, Sid threatens her and eventually fires her. Sid eventually realizes that Babe may have some justification for the strike. Sid begins romancing the President's secretary in order to gain access to the factory's books. He discovers that his boss has already been adding the pay increase into the price of his pajamas! Sid forces his boss' hand into giving the workers their raise, ending the strike, and salvaging his love life.

The Authors

Book by George Abbott and Richard Bissell
Music and Lyrics by Richard Adler and Jerry Ross

New York Run

May 13, 1954 – November 24, 1956, St. James Theater

The Song

"I'm Not At All In Love"

The girls are noticing that Babe and Sid seem to have some chemistry between them. Babe vehemently denies any attraction whatsoever.

Song type

Standard, Golden Age, Up Tempo, Comedy

Suggested 16-bar Audition Cut

m. 89, beat 3, to the end.

Have the accompanist give a bell tone starting pitch "A." Enter singing in tempo, *"But I'm not at all in love."* Although this cut is much larger than 16 bars, the quick tempo compensates for the additional measures.

Pal Joey

The Show

Setting: Chicago, late 1930s

Joey is an ambitious singer with a talent for sweet-talking the ladies. He romances the lovely but vulnerable Linda, who falls deeply for him. Yet when he meets the wealthy, older, and married Vera, a woman interested in bankrolling his career, he discards Linda. Vera smothers Joey, turning him into a kept man. At a chance encounter between Joey and Linda at a tailor shop, Vera reacts jealously. Joey's response to Linda's tears is nonchalant and dismissive. He is focused on getting his dream, his own nightclub. Immediately after his club Chez Joey opens, Joey becomes prey to the ruthless crook, Ludlow. Ludlow attempts to bring Linda in on a blackmail plot against Joey and Vera but she refuses. Linda reveals the plot to Vera who realizes she must give up Joey and end their affair. Linda and Joey meet one last time. As Linda exits, Joey notices another dame and follows her.

The Authors

Book by John O'Hara
Music by Richard Rogers
Lyrics by Lorenz Hart

New York Run

December 25, 1940 – November 29, 1941,
Ethel Barrymore Theatre, Shubert Theatre,
and St. James Theatre

The Song

"Bewitched, Bothered and Bewildered"

Although Joey has been rude and fresh with Vera, she still finds him charming. She ponders her feelings and plots to make him hers.

Song type

Standard Ballad, Dramatic

Suggested 16-bar Audition Cut

m. 37 to the end.

Have accompanist play the Dm7 chord on beat 1 of measure 37, emphasizing the starting pitch "B." Enter singing in tempo, *"Lost my heart, but what of it?"* Sing to the end.

Ragtime

The Show

Setting: In and around New York City, New Rochelle, Ellis Island, Lawrence, Massachusetts, and Atlantic City, New Jersey at the beginning of the 20th century

It is the dawn of a new century and America is bursting to change. Father has gone off adventuring, leaving Mother alone to look after the home and business. Although she is left behind, Mother wishes she could adventure also. When Sarah, a young, unmarried black girl abandons her child in Mother's garden, Mother brings them into her household, a brave but scandalous action. The father of the child, a jazz pianist named Coalhouse Walker finds Sarah and comes to New Rochelle weekly to court her. When Father returns, he is greatly disturbed by Mother's liberal actions. During one visit, racists vandalize Coalhouse's prized car. He seeks justice through the proper channels but is denied by the racist system. When Sarah tries to help by appealing to the President of the United States at a rally, she is attacked and beaten to death. In his anger, Coalhouse decides to seek justice as a vigilante.

Coalhouse takes over the Morgan Library, threatening to blow it up. Father offers his services to negotiate. Despite his assurances that Coalhouse will be taken into custody, Coalhouse is brutally gunned down by the police. As she adopts Sarah and Coalhouses' baby as her own, Mother realizes that she has gone on her own journey, a journey of new ideas towards equality and freedom and that she can never go back to the way it was before.

The Authors

Book by Terrance McNally
Music by Stephen Flaherty
Lyrics by Lynn Ahrens
Based on the novel *"Ragtime,"* by E.L. Doctorow.

New York Run

January 18, 1998 – January 16, 2000, Ford Center for the Performing Arts

The Song

"Your Daddy's Son"

Sarah, unmarried and frightened, abandoned her child, almost killing him. Grief-stricken and sorrowful, she sings to her child begging forgiveness and understanding for her terrible deed.

Song type

Contemporary Ballad, Dramatic

Suggested 16-bar Audition Cut

Option 1

m. 37 through 59 (highly dramatic belt).

Have the accompanist give a bell tone starting pitch "G" and/or the opening G minor arpeggio. Enter singing in tempo, *"Couldn't hear no music…"* Be sure to set tempo and volume (dramatic intensity) with your accompanist before starting. This is a highly charged song and you are entering in the middle of the dramatic action.

Option 2

m. 60 to the end (dramatic legit/mix).

Have the accompanist play measures 60-61 for an introduction. Enter singing in measure 62, *"Daddy played piano…"* Sing to the end.

Secret Garden

The Show

Setting: India and Misselthwaite Manor, North Yorkshire, England, 1906

Mary Lennox, a young spoiled rich girl, moves to England to live with her Uncle Archibald after her parents die during a cholera epidemic in India. Her Uncle Archibald is still grieving over the loss of his wife, Lilly, who died giving birth to their crippled son, Colin, who is kept isolated and hidden away in his room. Uncle Archibald does not welcome Mary easily as she looks like her Aunt Lilly and reminds him of that loss. In her loneliness, Mary befriends the chambermaid, Martha, and her brother, Dickson, who help her uncover a secret garden once lovingly tended by her Aunt Lilly but now lies abandoned and overgrown. When Archibald leaves because he cannot bear to be reminded of his loss, Mary nurtures both her cousin Colin and the untended garden, causing them to bloom and thrive. When Archibald returns and sees the changes Mary has brought about, he also blooms under Mary's love and embraces her as his own.

The Authors

Book and lyrics by Marsha Norman
Music by Lucy Simon
Based on the children's classic, *The Secret Garden* by Frances Hodgson Burnett.

New York Run

April 25, 1991 – January 3, 1993, St. James Theatre

The Song

"Hold On"

Angered by Mary's interference with Colin, Uncle Neville plans to send Mary away to a boarding school. Martha, the chambermaid, encourages Mary to "hold on," that things may still turn out well.

Song type
Contemporary Ballad, Dramatic

Suggested 16-bar Audition Cut
m. 46, beat 4, to the end.

Have the accompanist give a bell tone starting pitch "B." Begin singing in tempo, *"When you…"* Sing to the end.

Seussical

The Show

Setting: The Jungle of Nool, the present

Horton the Elephant makes a promise to protect and save the people of Whoville, a tiny town that exists on a speck of dust perched on a sprig of clover. Horton's best Who-friend is Jojo, a young boy who often gets in trouble for his creative "thinks." But sadly, only Horton can hear the Whos and as such, Horton's neighbors in the Jungle of Nool ridicule him for speaking to and trying to protect a seemingly insignificant speck of dust. Only his neighbor, the bird Gertrude McFuzz, believes in Horton and wants to help. Unfortunately, Horton doesn't notice her, which she believes is because she only has one feather in her tail. After many trials and long journeys, Whoville is saved by Horton's loyalty and one of Jojo's creative thinks. Horton finally notices Gertrude, and the entire Jungle believes in Horton.

The Authors

Book by Stephen Flaherty and Lynn Ahrens
Music by Stephen Flaherty
Lyrics by Lynn Ahrens
Conceived by Lynn Ahrens, Stephen Flaherty and Eric Idle.

Based on the beloved children's books by Dr. Seuss.

New York Run

November 30, 2000 – May 20, 2001, Richard Rodgers Theatre

The Song

"All For You"

Gertrude McFuzz rescues her friend, Horton the Elephant, after finally realizing true friendship is the key to his heart. She sings of the difficult trials that she has gone through to reach Horton.

Song type
Contemporary, Medium Tempo, Comedic

Suggested 16-bar Audition Cut
m. 42, beat 3, to the end.

Have the accompanist give a bell tone starting pitch "C." Enter singing in tempo, *"I sprained my little toe…"* Sing to the end.

Spring Awakening

The Show

Setting: a German province, 1891

Wendela is becoming a young woman. Confused by her changing body, her mother refuses to tell her anything except to cover up and be quiet. Melchior and his friend Moritz are also going through puberty with no guidance and extreme pressure to excel in school. Failure feels fraught with dire consequences. When Melchior and Wendela meet, they experience desire for the first time. With no guidance or understanding, they become lovers. Moritz fails at school. Having no perspective on life, he commits suicide. The school discovers writings by Melchior, which are attempts to instruct Moritz about sex. They blame Moritz's suicide on Melchior. Wendela is soon discovered pregnant, carrying Melchior's child. Melchior is sent to a reformatory and Wendela is forced into a backstreet abortion. Melchior escapes the reformatory only to discover that Wendela has died. Melchior pledges never to forget his lost love and dear friend.

The Authors

Book and Lyrics by Steven Sater
Music by Duncan Sheik
Based on the Play "Spring Awakening"
by Frank Wedekind.

New York Run

December 10, 2006 – January 18, 2009
Eugene O'Neill Theatre

The Songs

"Mama Who Bore Me"

Wendela is questioning the changes in her body. Her mother's refusal to give her guidance has left her vulnerable and without direction.

Song type

Contemporary Ballad, Dramatic

Suggested 16-bar Audition Cut

m. 11 to the end.

Have the accompanist give a bell tone starting pitch "A," (pickup in m. 10). Enter singing in tempo, *"Some pray that one day…"* Sing to the end.

"Whispering"

Wendela has died from her abortion. From beyond the grave, she watches her funeral and her lover, Melchior's grief.

Song type

Contemporary Ballad, Dramatic

Suggested 16-bar Audition Cut

m. 48 to the end.

Have accompanist play the starting pitches "E, F#" (pickups in m. 47). Enter singing in tempo, *"Had a sweetheart…."* Sing to the end.

St. Louis Woman

The Show

Setting: St. Louis, Missouri, 1891

Little Augie is a jockey on a hot winning streak and in love with Della, the belle of St. Louis. Unfortunately she is involved with the violent and faithless Bigalow Brown. Della leaves Brown and falls in love with Augie. They make plans to marry. Brown's former mistress, Lila is still in love with him and wants him back. One day, while Augie is racing, Brown tracks down Della and beats her. Lila arrives, begging for Brown to return to her. He refuses. When Augie returns, a shot is fired. Brown believes Augie has shot him and curses him. At Brown's funeral, Lila confesses to the murder. Despite the truth, Augie's winning streak is at an end. Della blames herself for Augie's misfortune. She leaves him with a lie, saying he can no longer provide her with the life she wants. Augie learns of Della's lie. To prove the curse to be mumbo-jumbo, he must win his next race. He wins and Della and Augie happily reunite.

The Authors

Book by Arna Bontemps and Countee Cullen
Music by Harold Arlen
Lyrics by Johnny Mercer
Based on the novel, *"God Sends Sunday,"*
by Arna Bontemps.

New York Run

March 30, 1946 – July 6, 1946, Martin Beck Theatre

The Song

"I Had Myself a True Love"

Lila is still in love with Bigalow Brown. She tells the story of her loss and her sorrow.

Song type

Standard, Golden Age, Ballad, Dramatic

Suggested 16-bar Audition Cut

Option 1 (lyrical legit)

m. 1 through m. 20.

Have accompanist play the introduction from measure 1. Enter singing, *"I had myself a true love."* End at measure 20, *"An' that's the way I live thru the day."*

Option 2 (dramatic)

m. 44, beat 4, to the end.

Have the accompanist give a bell tone starting pitch "C." Enter in tempo singing, *"Where is he while I watch…."* Be sure to set tempo and volume (dramatic intensity) with your accompanist before starting. You are entering in the middle of a highly charged dramatic moment in the song.

Thoroughly Modern Millie

The Show

Setting: New York City, 1922

Millie arrives in Manhattan ready to take the world by storm. She moves into the Hotel Priscilla, a boarding house for aspiring actresses run by the suspicious Mrs. Meers which is really a front for Mrs. Meers' white slavery operation, selling off young orphaned actresses. When the young, orphaned Miss Dorothy enters, she and Millie become fast friends. Millie lands a position as stenographer to the single and wealthy Trevor Graydon, also hoping to land him as a rich husband. The girls go out to celebrate and run into the slick bachelor, Jimmy Smith. Jimmy learns of Millie's marriage plans and decides Millie would be great to date. She won't interrupt his bachelor ways. Jimmy is eventually confronted by Muzzy, a grand New York society dame, regarding his true feelings for Millie. He's in love. Millie also recognizes she loves Jimmy. However, later that night Millie sees Jimmy sneaking out of Dorothy's room at the Hotel Priscilla! Jealously hurt, Millie doubles her efforts to snag Graydon despite Jimmy's romantic overtures. Muzzy again intervenes and teaches Millie to follow her heart. We then learn that Jimmy is Muzzy's son and Dorothy her daughter. But where is Dorothy? Last minute hi-jinks save Miss Dorothy from Mrs. Meers' clutches and Miss Dorothy finds true love in her rescuer, Ching Ho, Mrs. Meers' houseboy!

The Authors

Book by Richard Henry Morris and Dick Scanlon
Music by Jeanine Tesori
Lyrics by Dick Scanlan
Based on the film "Thoroughly Modern Millie."

New York Run

April 18, 2002 – June 20, 2004, Marquis Theatre

The Song

"Gimme, Gimme"

Millie confesses to her society friend, Muzzy, that despite Millie's efforts to marry a rich man, she has fallen in love with the poor Jimmy Smith. Muzzy tells Millie that she made the same choice, married for love, and life turned out wonderful. Now it is time for Millie to make her choice.

Song type
Contemporary, Medium Tempo, Dramatic (Belt)

Suggested 16-bar Audition Cut
m. 86 to the end.

Have the accompanist give a starting pitch "A." Enter singing in tempo, *"Here I am, Saint Valentine."* Sing to the end. Be sure to set opening tempo and tempo change in measure 90 with your accompanist.

The Wiz

The Show

Setting: Kansas and various locales in the Land of Oz, the present

A tornado blows Dorothy all the way from Kansas to the Land of Oz. Her house lands on top of the Wicked Witch of the East, killing her. She is proclaimed a hero. Dorothy wants to return home. She is told that the Wizard in the Emerald City is the only one who can help her. She is given the witch's magic shoes as protection and sets off. On her journey she befriends a Scarecrow who wishes for brains, a Tinman who wishes for a heart, and a Lion who wishes for courage. When they finally meet the Wiz, he is terrifying. He agrees to grant their wishes if they kill the Wicked Witch of the West. Dorothy is captured but quickly vanquishes the Wicked Witch by throwing water at her, causing her to melt. They return to the Emerald City and discover that the Wizard is just a conman from Nebraska, blown into Oz in a hot air balloon. He agrees to take Dorothy back in his balloon but is again blown away. Dorothy is left despondent until the Good Witch of the South reveals that Dorothy always had it within her power to go home. She only has to wish and click her heels three times.

The Authors

Book by William F. Brown
Music and lyrics by Charlie Smalls
Adapted from "The Wonderful Wizard of Oz"
by L. Frank Baum.

New York Run

January 5, 1975 – January 28, 1979, Majestic Theatre and Broadway Theatre

The Song

"Home"

Dorothy has finally learned that the way home is simple, to just believe, wish her way home, and click her heels three times. As she promises her friends she will return, she sings of where she truly longs to be.

Song type
Contemporary Ballad, Pop, Dramatic (Mix/Belt)

Suggested 16-bar Audition Cut
m. 54 to the end.

Have accompanist begin playing an introduction at measure 53. Enter singing, *"Living here in this brand new world...."* Sing to the end.

THE SONGS

A LITTLE BRAINS, A LITTLE TALENT

(from "Damn Yankees")

Words and Music by
RICHARD ADLER and JERRY ROSS

© 1955 FRANK MUSIC CORP.
Copyright Renewed and Assigned to J & J ROSS CO. and LAKSHMI PUJA MUSIC LTD.
All Rights Administered by THE SONGWRITERS GUILD OF AMERICA
All Rights Reserved

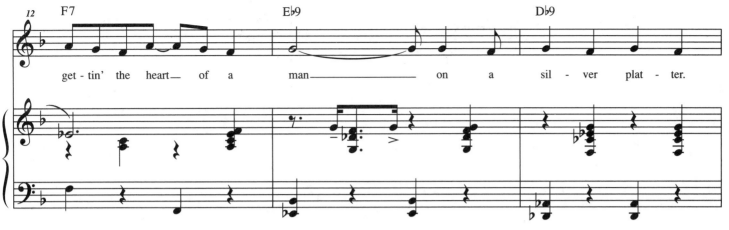

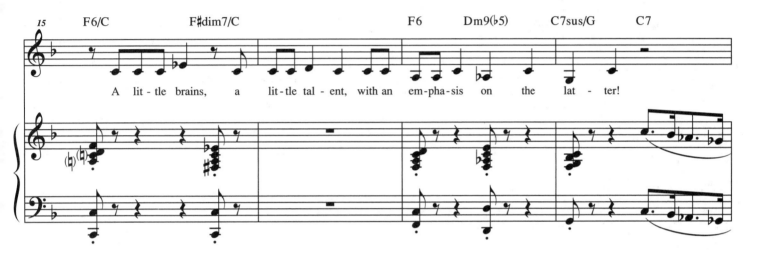

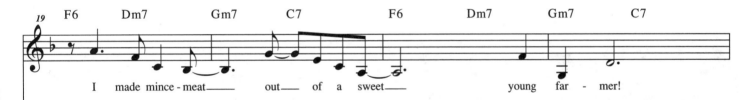

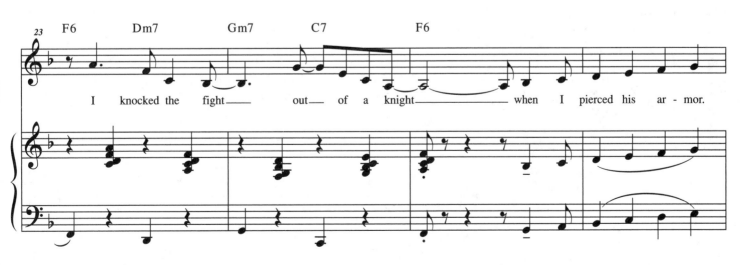

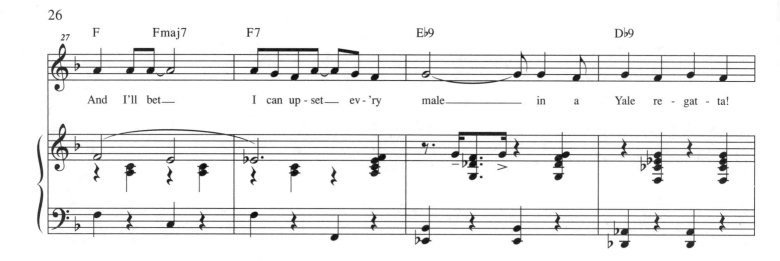

And I'll bet— I can up-set— ev-'ry male———— in a Yale re-gat-ta!

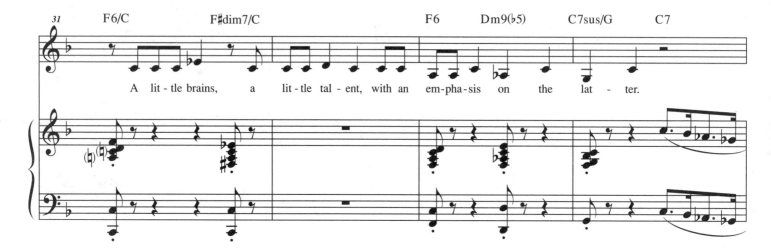

A lit-tle brains, a lit-tle tal-ent, with an em-pha-sis on the lat-ter.

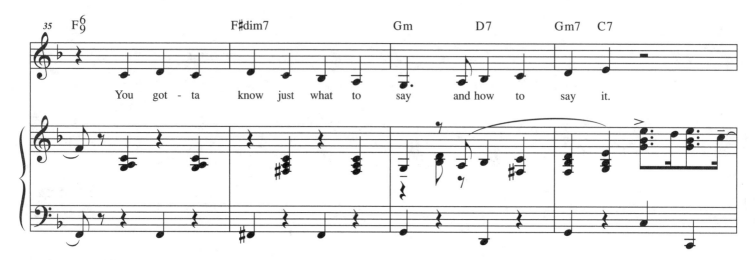

You got-ta know just what to say and how to say it.

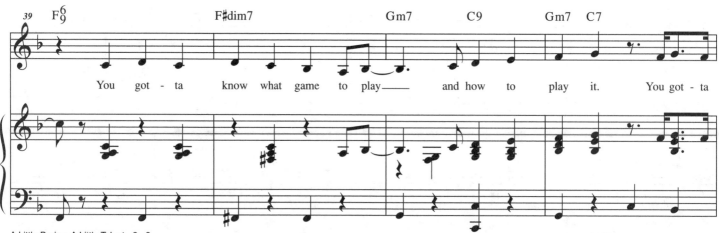

You got-ta know what game to play— and how to play it. You got-ta

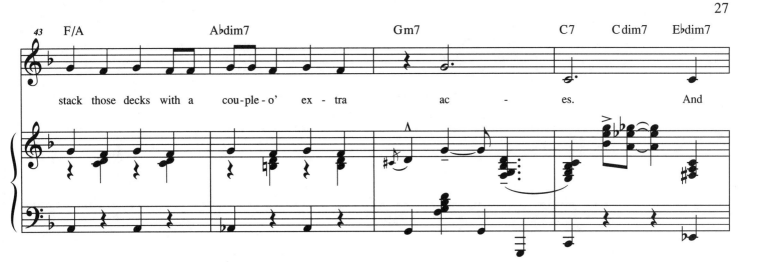

stack those decks with a cou-ple - o' ex - tra ac - es. And

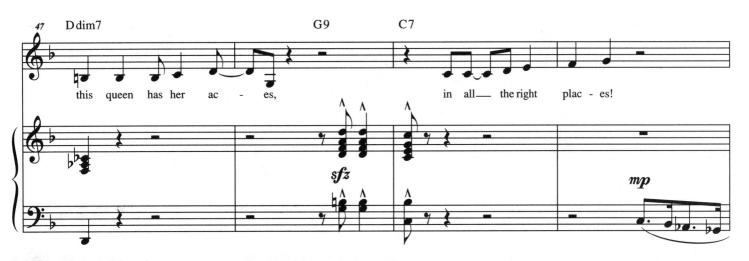

this queen has her ac - es, in all— the right plac - es!

I've done much more—— than— that old bore—— De - li - lah!

I took the curl—— out— of the hair—— of a mil - lion - aire. There

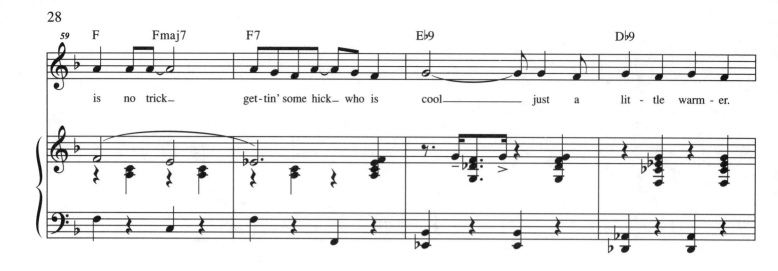

is no trick— get-tin' some hick— who is cool———— just a lit-tle warm-er.

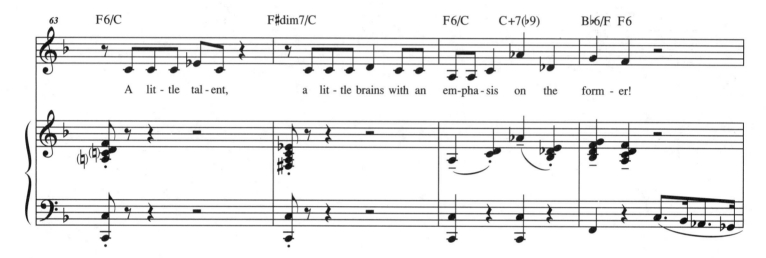

A lit-tle tal-ent, a lit-tle brains with an em-pha-sis on the form-er!

Split up a home—— way— up in Nome,— A - las - ka!

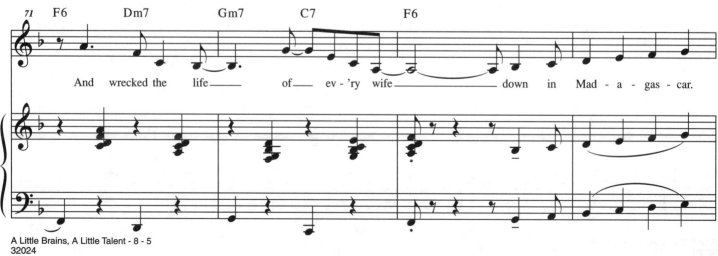

And wrecked the life——— of—— ev-'ry wife——— down in Mad - a - gas - car.

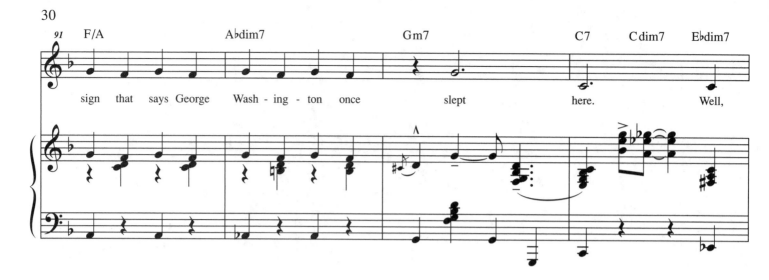

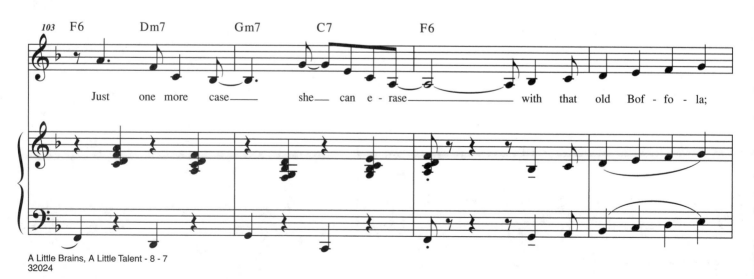

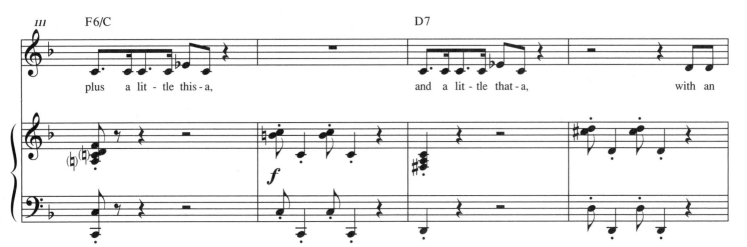

ALL FOR YOU
(from "Seussical the Musical")

Lyrics by
LYNN AHRENS

Music by
STEPHEN FLAHERTY

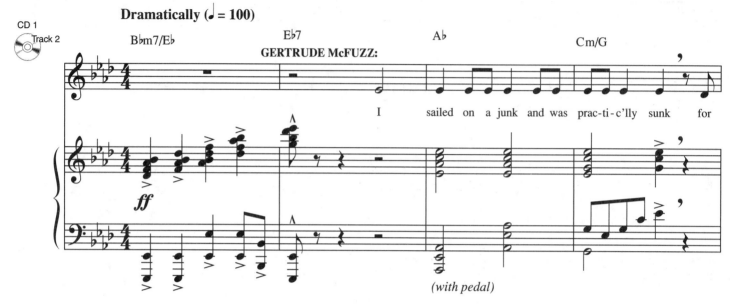

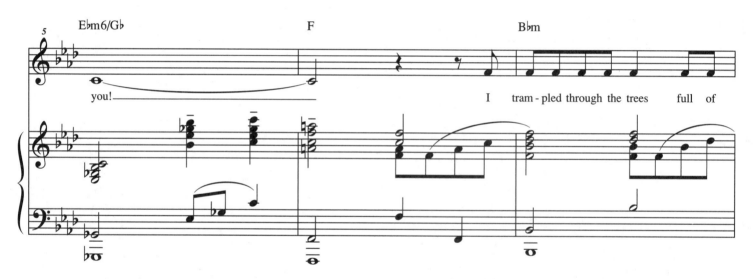

© 2001 WB MUSIC CORP., PEN AND PERSEVERANCE and HILLSDALE MUSIC, INC.
All Rights Administered by WB MUSIC CORP.
All Rights Reserved

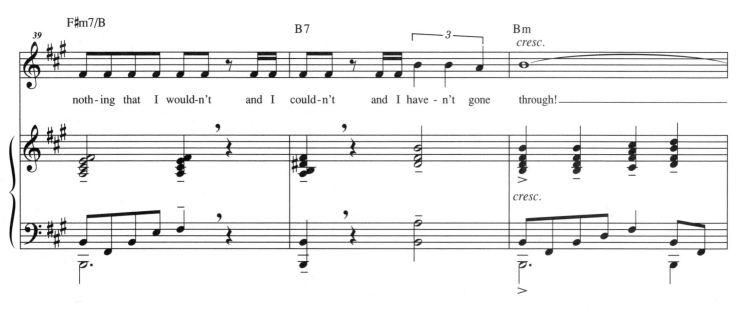

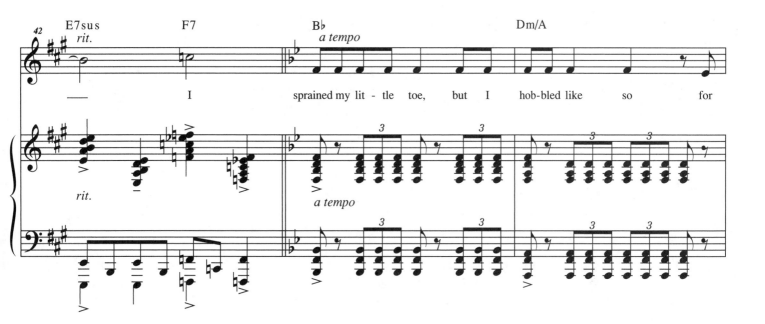

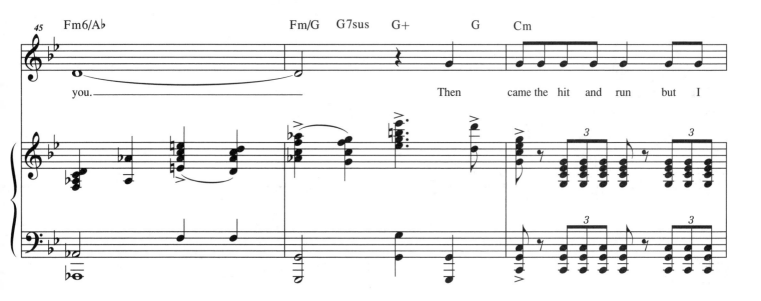

ALWAYS TRUE TO YOU IN MY FASHION

(from "Kiss Me Kate")

Words and Music by
COLE PORTER

© 1948 by COLE PORTER
Copyright Renewed and Assigned to JOHN F. WHARTON,
Trustee of the COLE PORTER MUSICAL AND LITERARY PROPERTY TRUSTS.
CHAPPELL & CO., INC. Owner of Publication and Allied Rights Throughout the World
All Rights Reserved

Always True to You in My Fashion - 5 - 1
32024

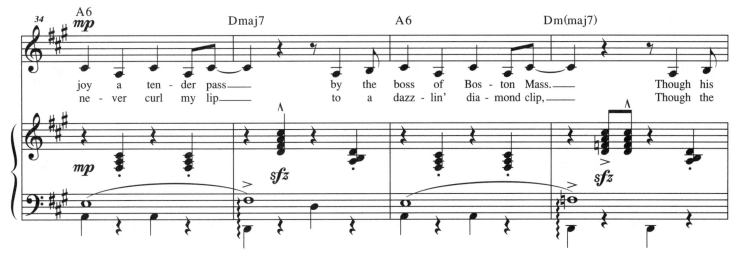

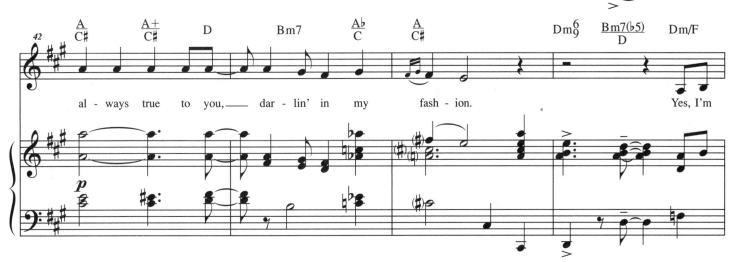

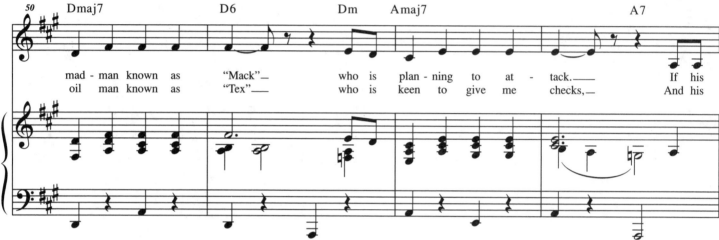

ASTONISHING

(from "Little Women")

Lyrics by
MINDI DICKSTEIN

Music by
JASON HOWLAND

© 2005 CHERRY RIVER MUSIC CO. (BMI), HOWLAND MUSIC (BMI) and LITTLE ESKY PUBLISHING (ASCAP)
This Arrangement © 2008 CHERRY RIVER MUSIC CO. (BMI), HOWLAND MUSIC (BMI)
and LITTLE ESKY PUBLISHING (ASCAP)
Worldwide Rights for HOWLAND MUSIC Administered by CHERRY RIVER MUSIC CO.
Worldwide Rights for LITTLE ESKY PUBLISHING Administered by CHERRY LANE MUSIC PUBLISHING COMPANY, INC.
All Rights Reserved   Used by Permission

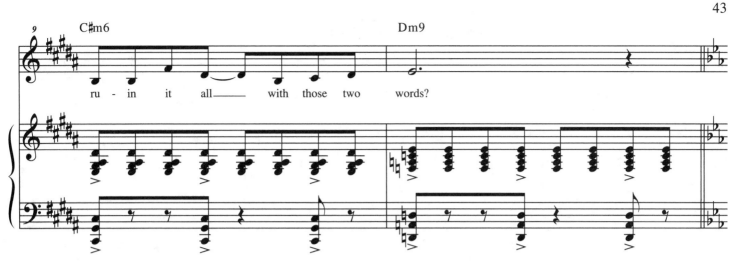

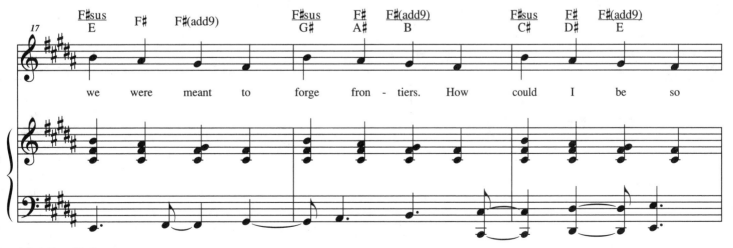

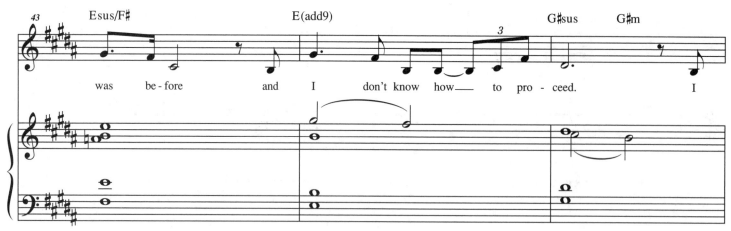

was be-fore and I don't know how— to pro-ceed. I

In 4

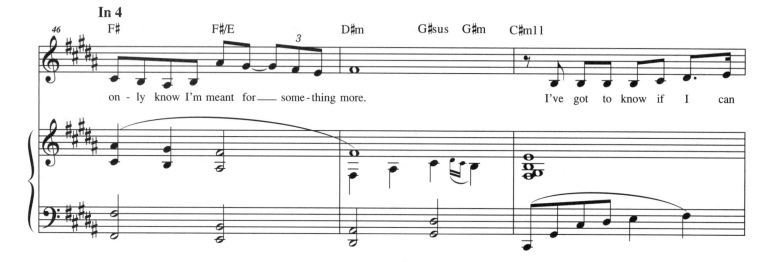

on-ly know I'm meant for— some-thing more. I've got to know if I can

be a - ston-ish - ing.— There's a

life that I am meant to lead, a-live like noth-ing— I have

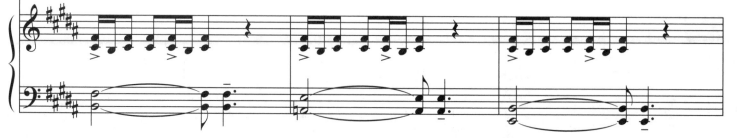

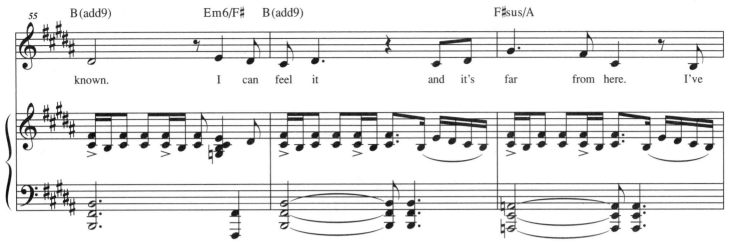

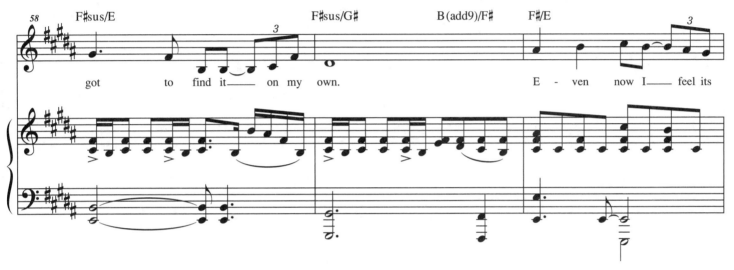

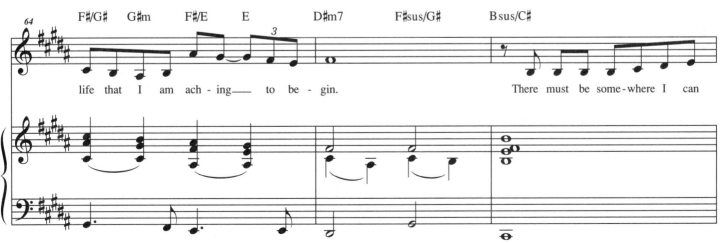

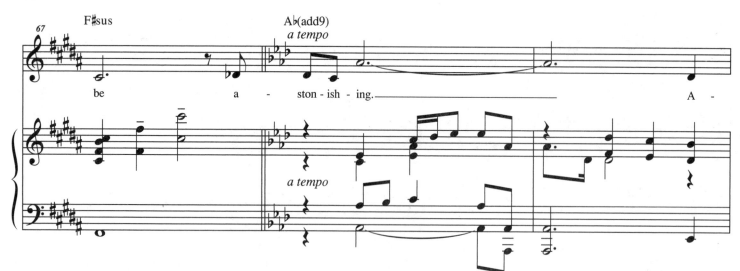

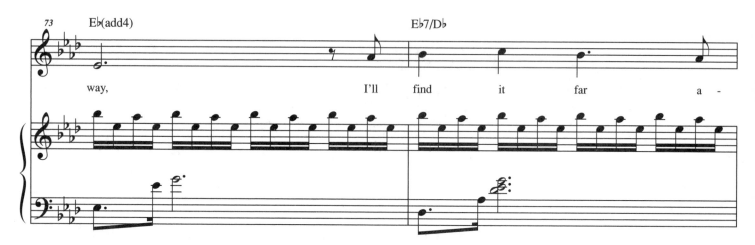

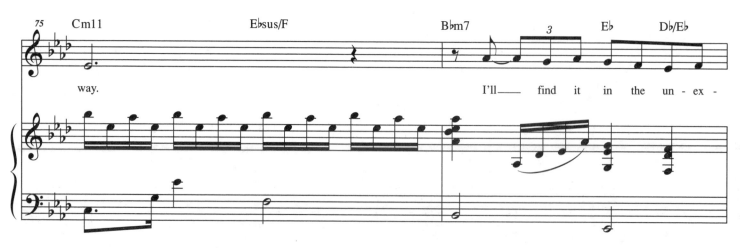

I'll shout and start a ri - ot, be an - y - thing but qui - et. Chris - to - pher Co - lum - bus, I'll be a - ston - ish - ing. A -

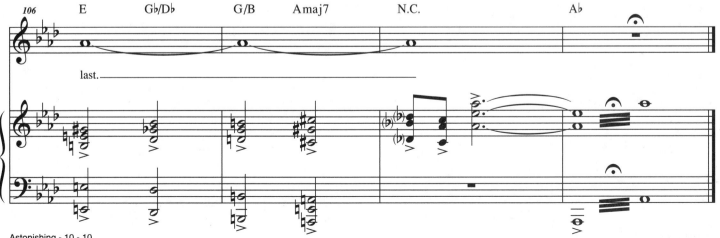

ston - ish - ing,_____ a - ston-ish - ing_____ at last._____

BEWITCHED, BOTHERED and BEWILDERED

(from "Pal Joey")

Words by
LORENZ HART

Music by
RICHARD RODGERS

Bewitched, Bothered and Bewildered - 3 - 1
32024

© 1941 (Renewed) CHAPPELL & CO., INC.
Rights for Extended Renewal Term in U.S. Controlled by WB MUSIC CORP. and WILLIAMSON MUSIC CO.
All Rights Reserved

54

Bewitched, Bothered and Bewildered - 3 - 3
32024

BOY WANTED

(from "My One and Only")

Lyrics by
ARTHUR FRANCIS

Music by
GEORGE GERSHWIN

CD 1
Track 6

Moderato

EDITH:

I've just fin-ished writ-ing an ad-ver-tise-ment ____ call-ing for ____ a boy. ____ No half-heart-ed Ro-me-o or flirt is meant, ____ that's the kind I'd not ____ em-ploy, ____ though

© 1924 (Renewed) WB MUSIC CORP.
All Rights Reserved

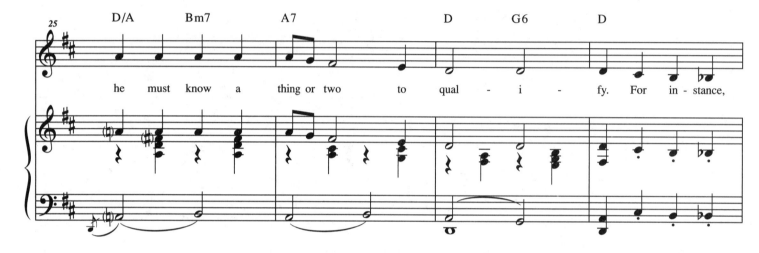

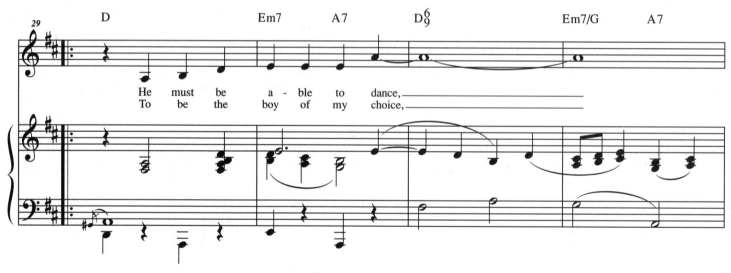

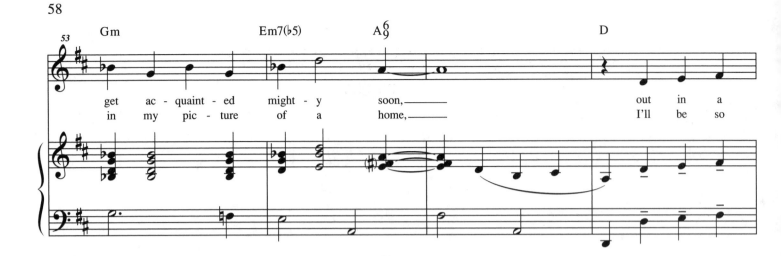

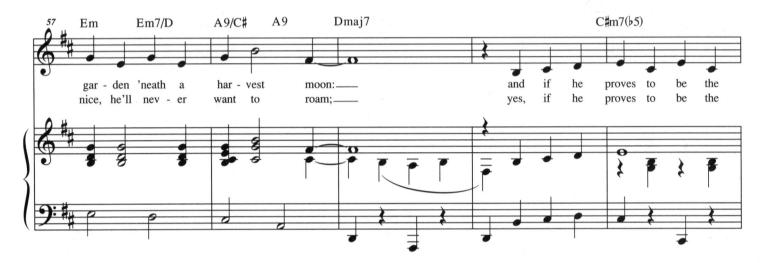

DON'T RAIN ON MY PARADE

(from "Funny Girl")

Words by
BOB MERRILL

Music by
JULE STYNE

© 1964 (Renewed) by BOB MERRILL and JULE STYNE
Publication and Allied Rights Assigned to WONDERFUL MUSIC, INC.
and Administered by CHAPPELL & CO., INC.
All Rights Reserved

Don't Rain on My Parade - 8 - 1
32024

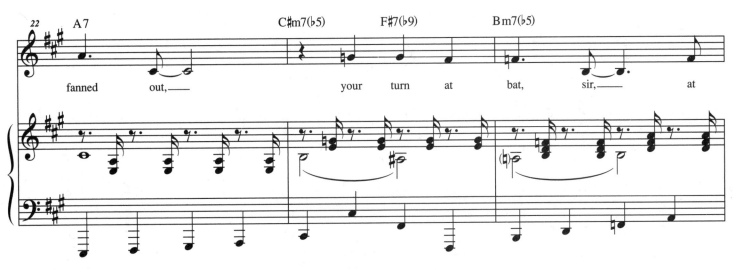

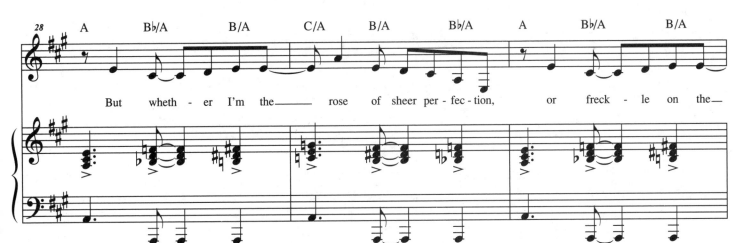

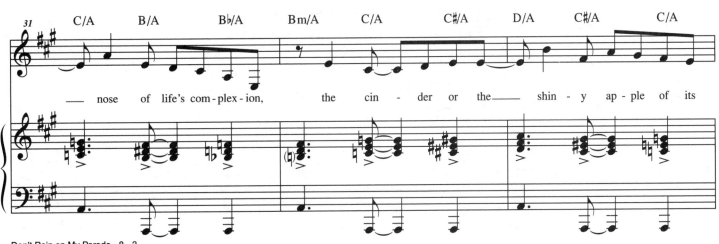

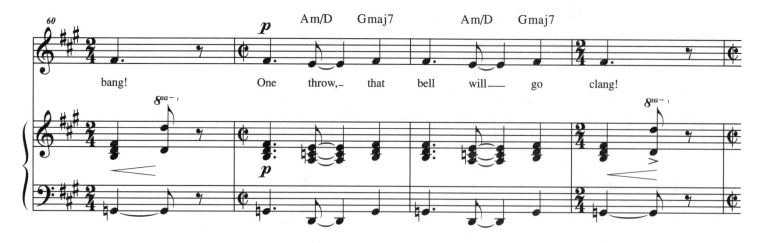

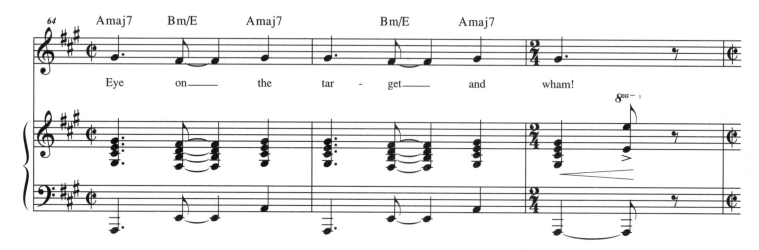

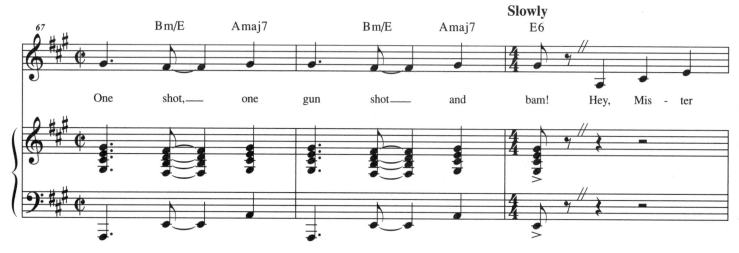

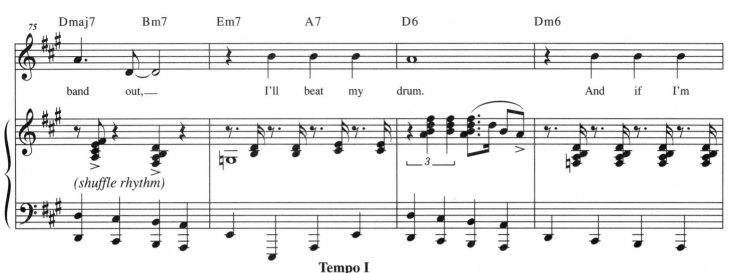

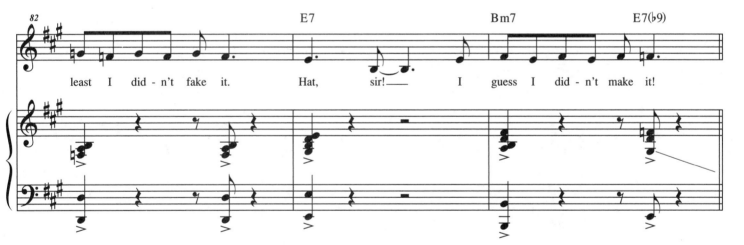

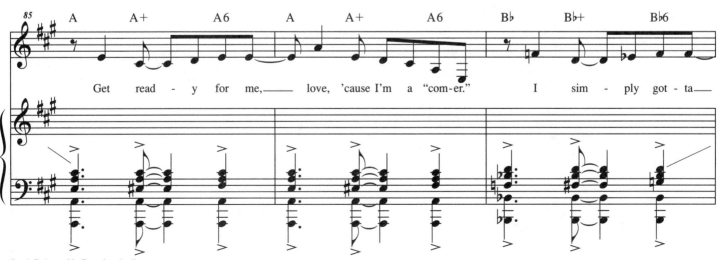

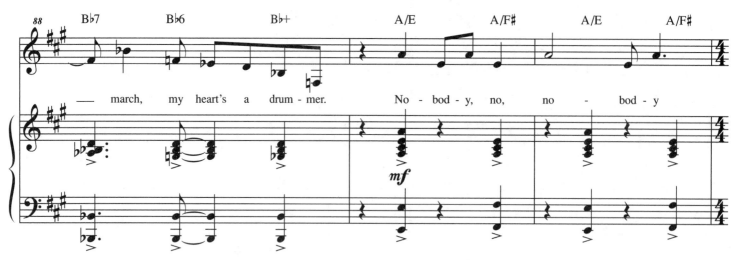

march, my heart's a drum - mer. No - bod - y, no, no - bod - y

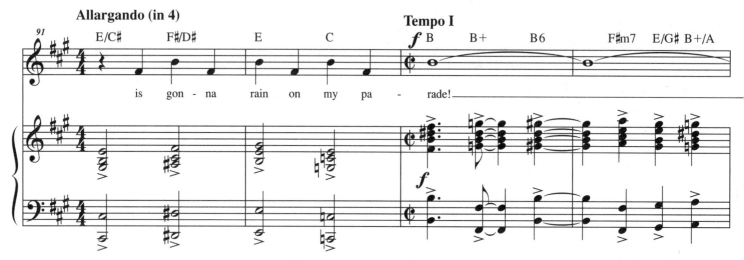

Allargando (in 4)

Tempo I

is gon - na rain on my pa - rade! ___

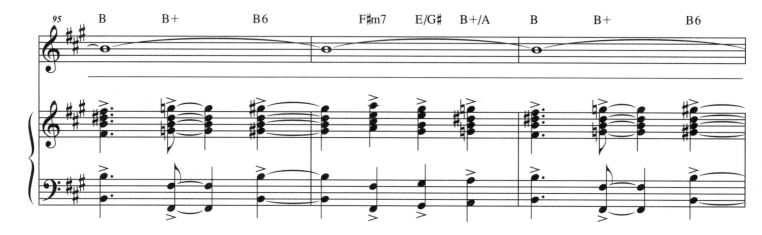

GIMME GIMME
(from "Thoroughly Modern Millie")

Lyrics by
DICK SCANLAN

Music by
JEANINE TESORI

© 2001 THAT'S MUSIC TO MY EARS LTD. and THOROUGHLY MODERN MUSIC PUBLISHING CO.
This Arrangement © 2008 THAT'S MUSIC TO MY EARS LTD. and THOROUGHLY MODERN MUSIC PUBLISHING CO.
All Rights Reserved   Used by Permission

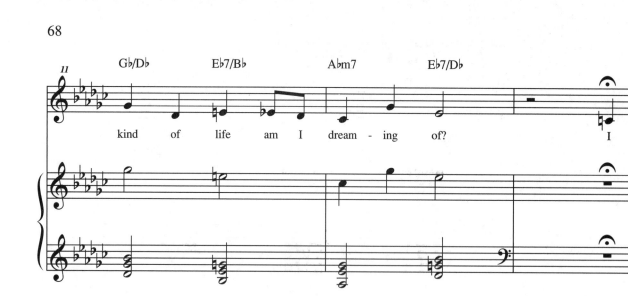

kind of life am I dream-ing of? I say:

Moderately slow

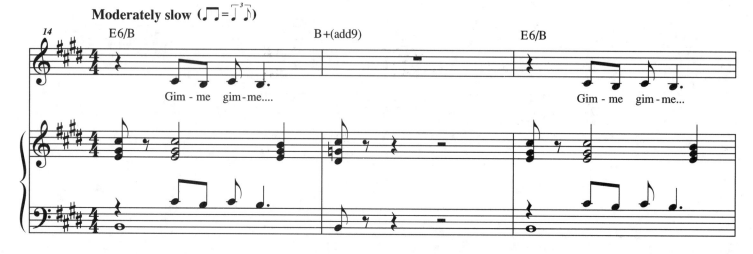

Gim-me gim-me.... Gim-me gim-me...

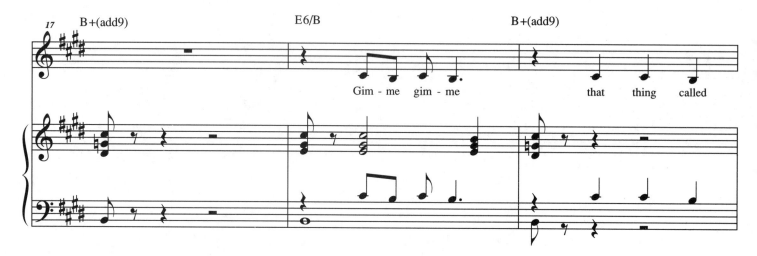

Gim-me gim-me that thing called

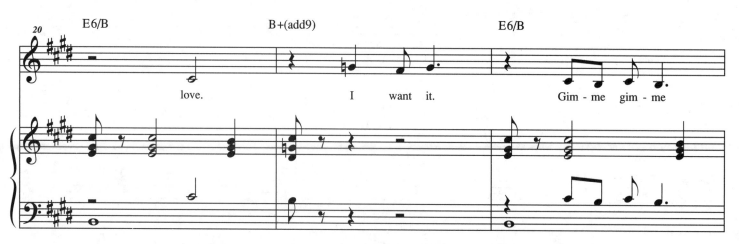

love. I want it. Gim-me gim-me

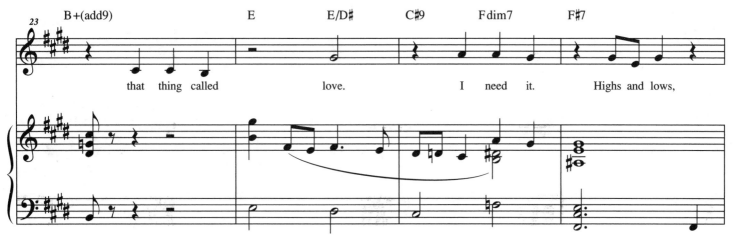

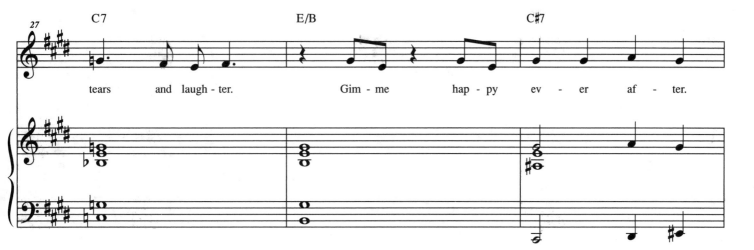

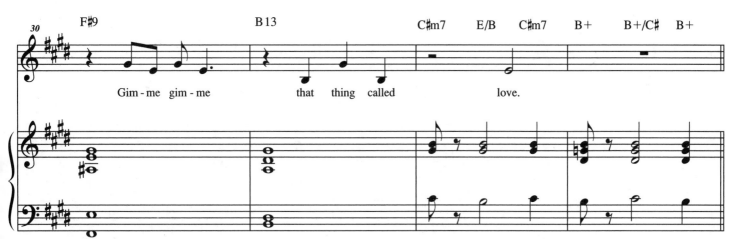

Moderately, with more confidence

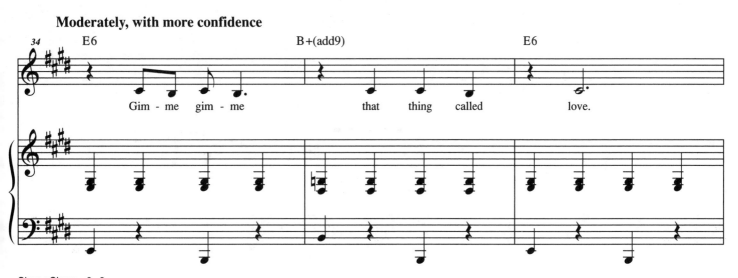

HOLD ON

(from "The Secret Garden")

Lyrics by
MARSHA NORMAN

Music by
LUCY SIMON

Resolutely, with pulse (♩ = 80)

CD 1
Track 9

MARTHA:

What you've got to do is fin - ish

(with pedal)

what you have be - gun.   I don't know just how, but it's not   o - ver 'til you've won.   When you

resolutely
a tempo

see the storm is com - in',   see the light-'ning part the skies,   it's too late to run.   There's

a tempo

© 1991, 1992 ABCDE PUBLISHING LTD. and CALOUGIE MUSIC
All Rights Administered by WB MUSIC CORP.
All Rights Reserved

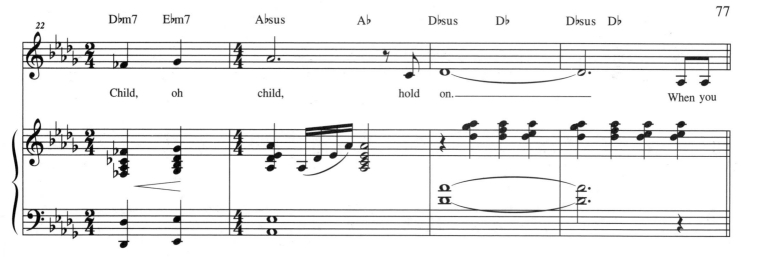

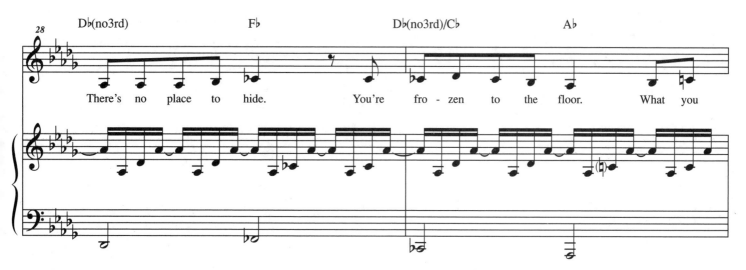

C#m   G#m   A   F#7sus   F#

do then is you tell your-self to wait it out. You say, "It's this

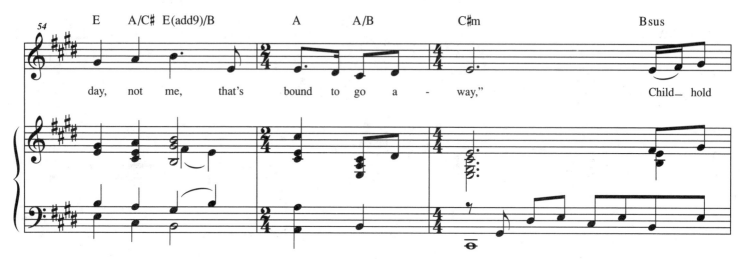

E   A/C#   E(add9)/B   A   A/B   C#m   Bsus

day, not me, that's bound to go a-way," Child— hold

E/F#   F#7   E   A/C#   E(add9)/B   A/F#   Amaj7/G#   F#m/A   A/B

on. It's this day not you that's bound to go a-

Esus   E   D6/E   E(add9)   E

rall.

way.

rall.

(with pedal)

HOME
(from "The Wiz")

Words and Music by
CHARLIE SMALLS

© 1974 (Renewed) WARNER-TAMERLANE PUBLISHING CORP.
All Rights Reserved

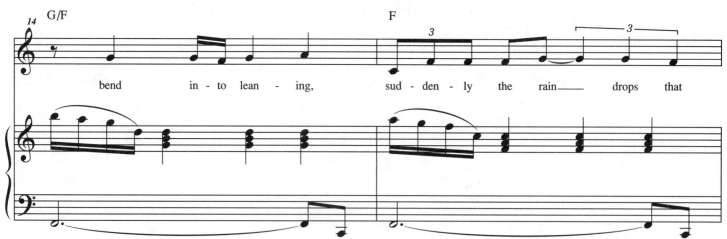

bend in - to lean - ing, sud - den - ly the rain___ drops that

fall_____ have a mean-ing. Sprink - lin' the scene_____

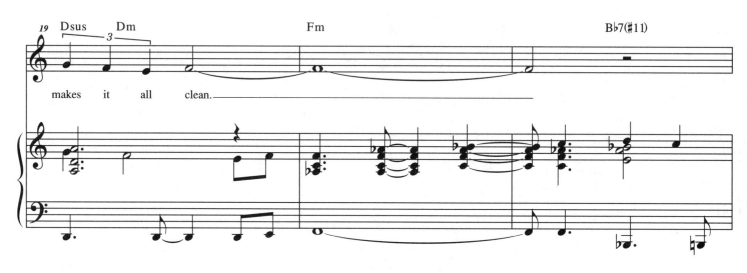

makes it all clean._____

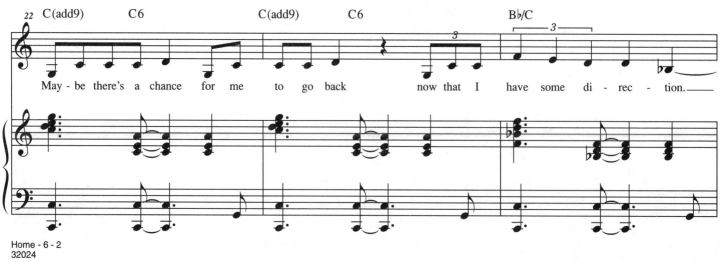

May - be there's a chance for me to go back now that I have some di - rec - tion.___

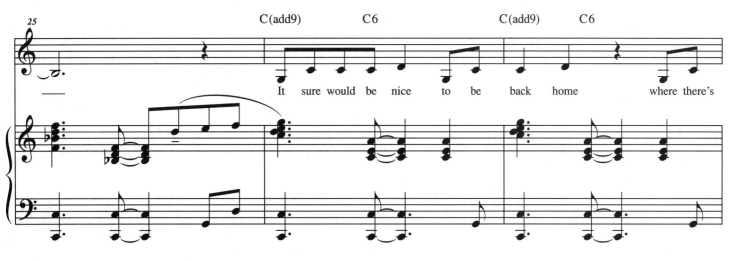

It sure would be nice to be back home where there's

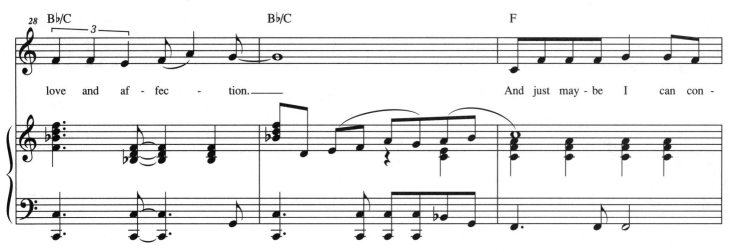

love and af-fec - tion. And just may-be I can con-

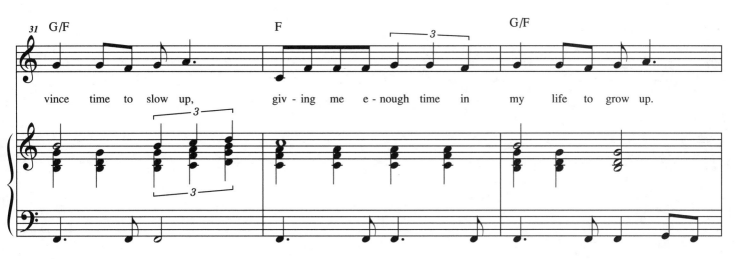

vince time to slow up, giv-ing me e-nough time in my life to grow up.

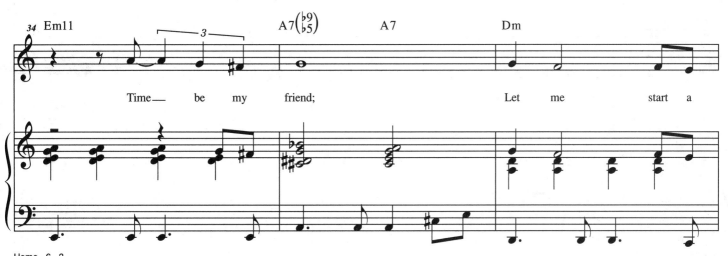

Time be my friend; Let me start a

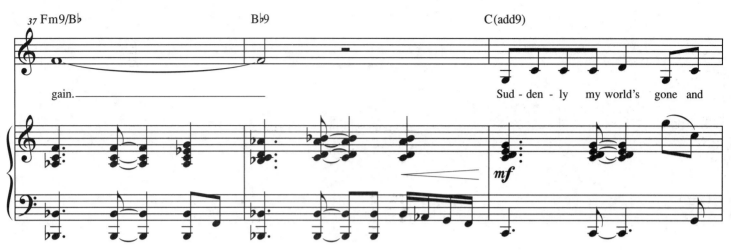

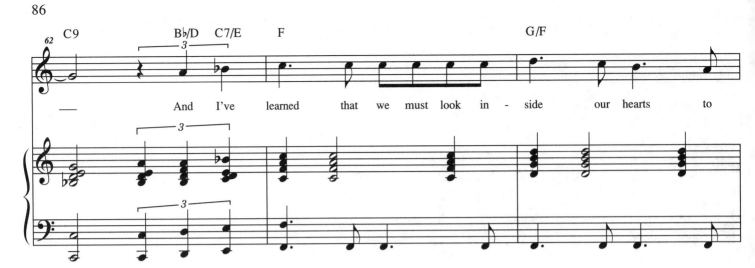

And I've learned that we must look in - side our hearts to

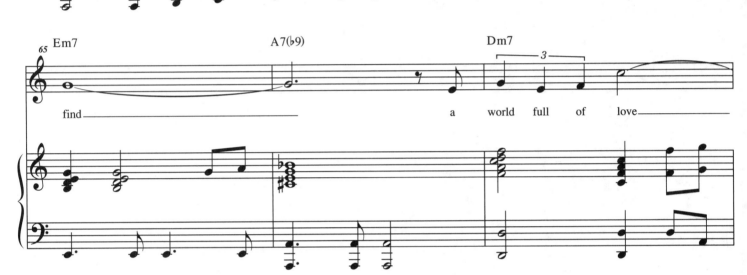

find _____ a world full of love _____

_____ like yours, like mine, _____ like

home. _____

HOW ARE THINGS IN GLOCCA MORRA?

(from "Finian's Rainbow")

Words by
E.Y. HARBURG

Music by
BURTON LANE

© 1946 (Renewed) CHAPPELL & CO., INC. and GLOCCA MORRA MUSIC CORP.
All Rights Reserved

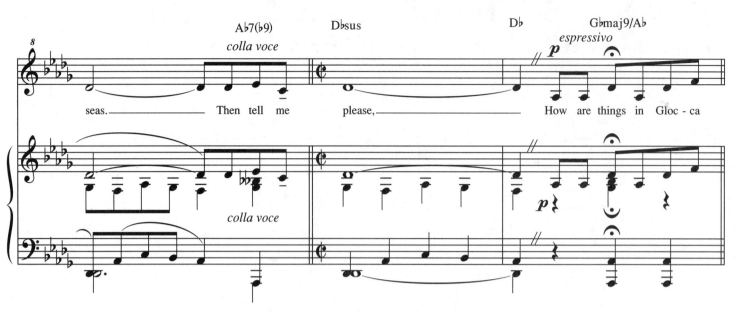

Lento espressivo ($\quad$ = 56)

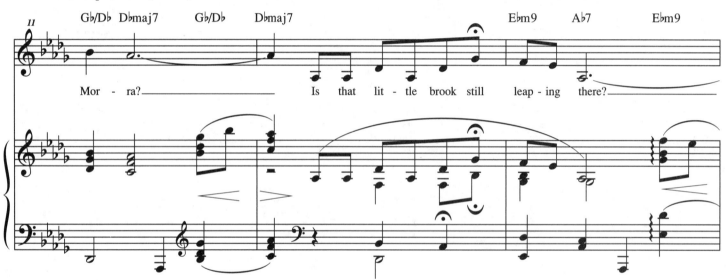

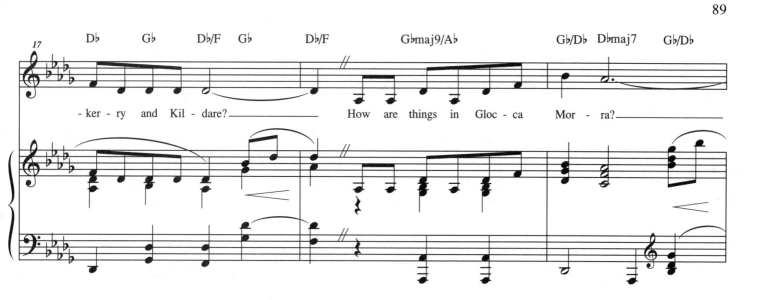

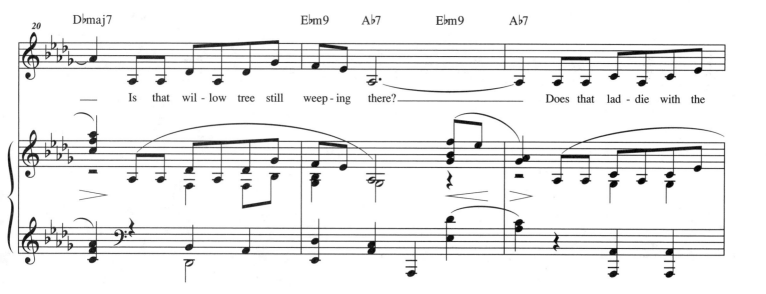

90

I HAD MYSELF A TRUE LOVE

(from "St. Louis Woman")

Words by
JOHNNY MERCER

Music by
HAROLD ARLEN

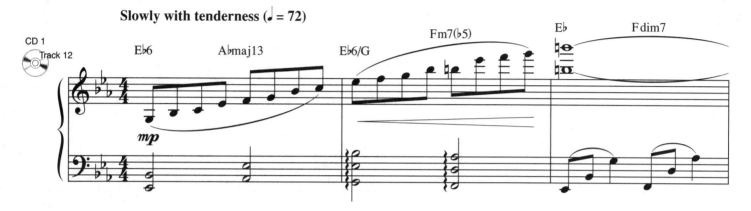

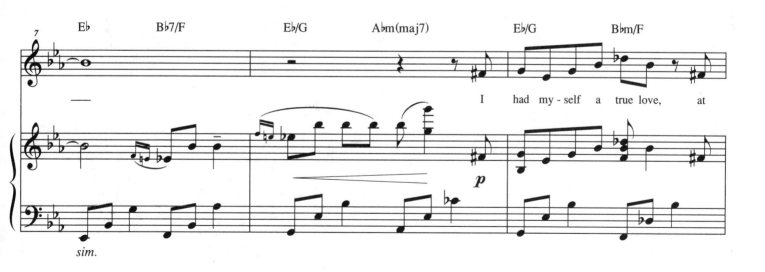

© 1946 (Renewed) THE JOHNNY MERCER FOUNDATION and S.A. MUSIC CO.
All Rights for THE JOHNNY MERCER FOUNDATION Administered by WB MUSIC CORP.
All Rights Reserved

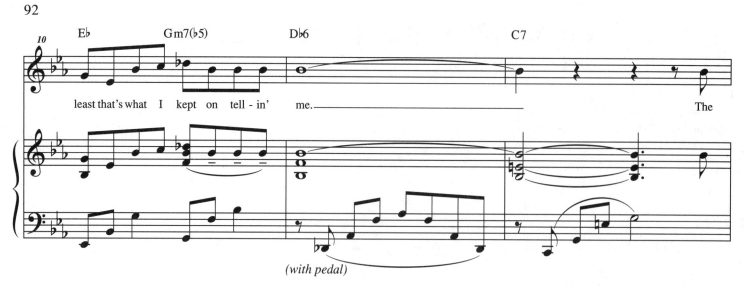

least that's what I kept on tell-in' me._____ The

first thing in the morn-in'_____ I still try to think up a way_____ to be with him,

some part of the eve-nin'. An' that's the way I live thru the day. "She

Swing eighths

had her-self a true love, but now he's gone an' left her for good."_____

sim.

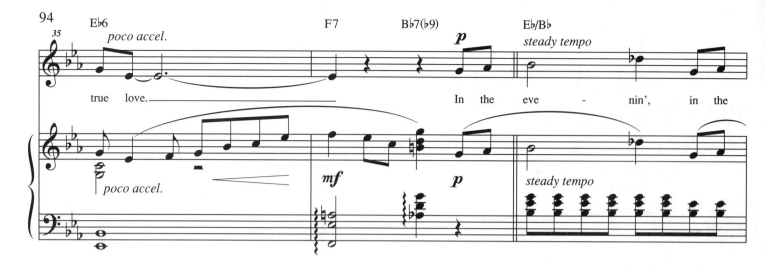

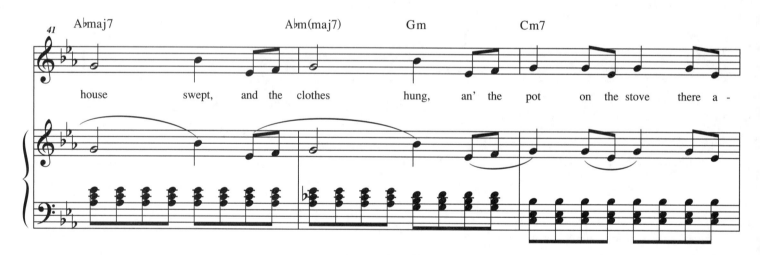

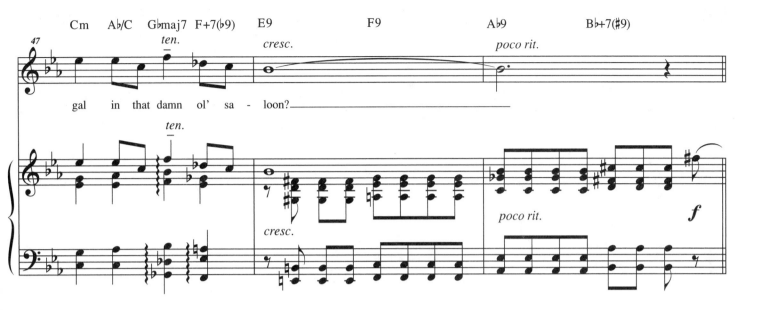

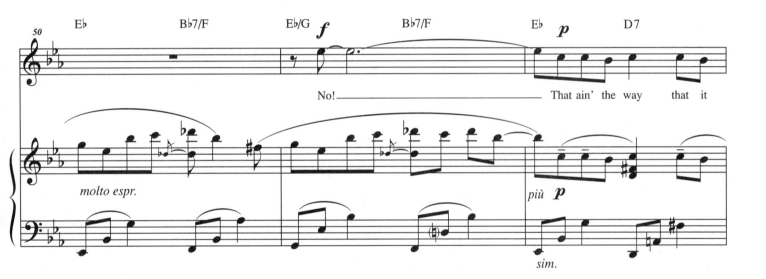

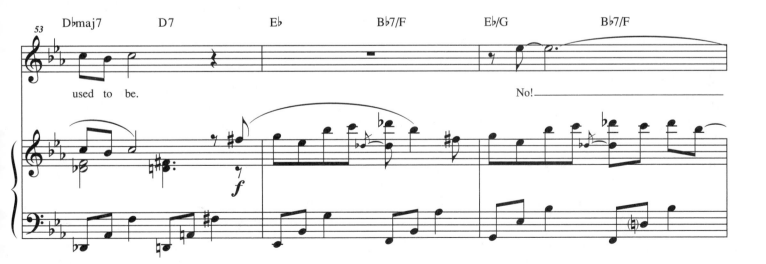

I Had Myself a True Love - 6 - 5
32024

I SPEAK SIX LANGUAGES

(from "The 25th Annual Putnam County Spelling Bee")

Words and Music by
WILLIAM FINN

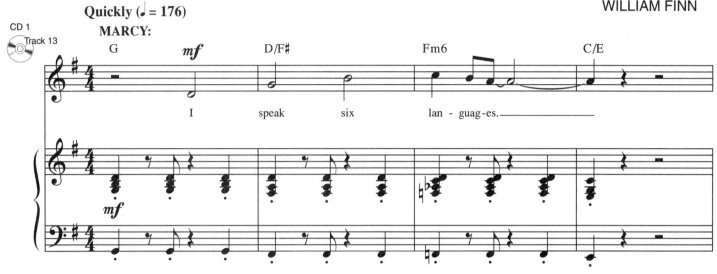

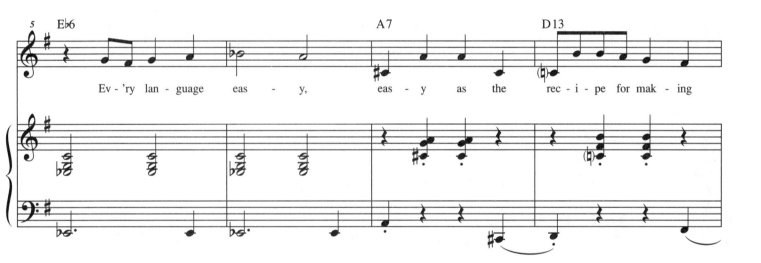

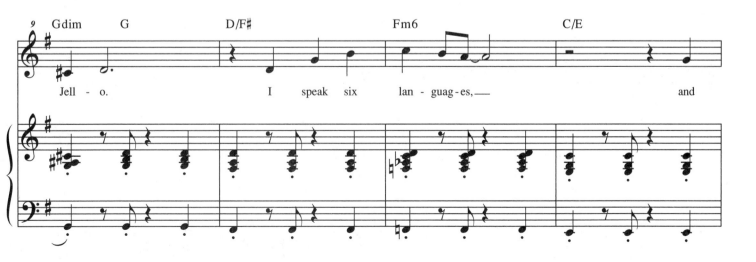

© 2005 WB MUSIC CORP. and IPSY PIPSY MUSIC
All Rights Administered by WB MUSIC CORP.
All Rights Reserved

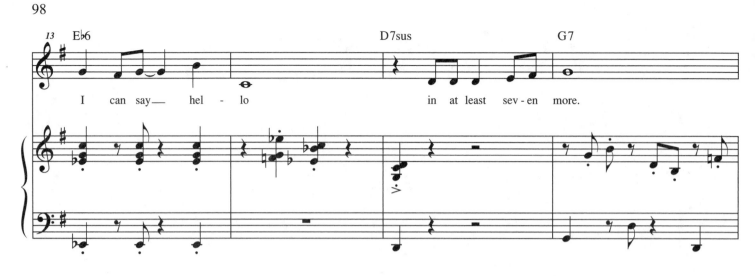

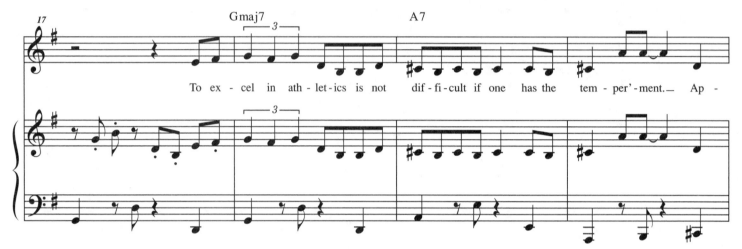

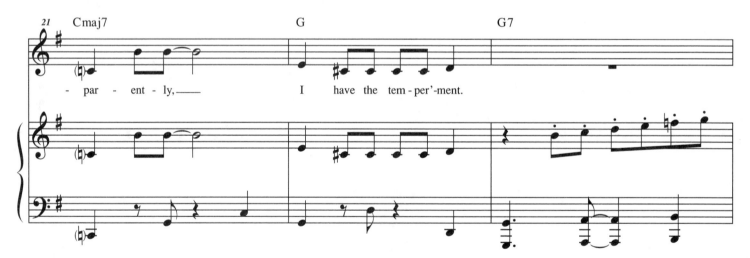

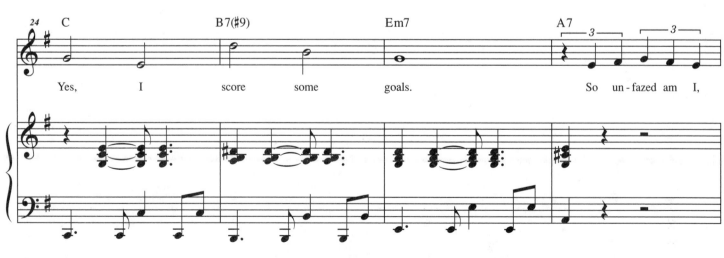

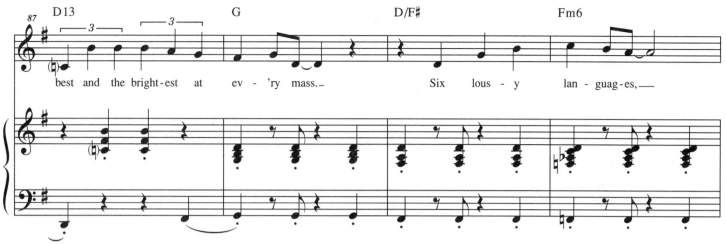

best and the bright-est at ev-'ry mass.— Six lous-y lan-guag-es,—

and for my height, I'm— the light-est of the girls in my

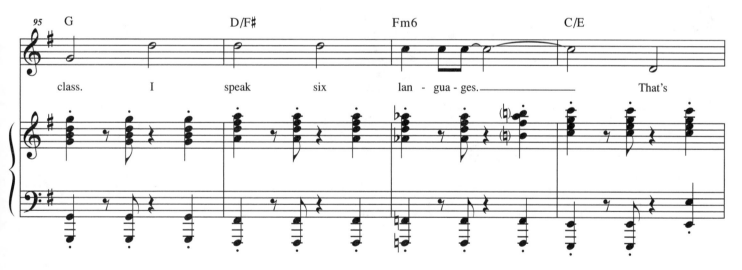

class. I speak six lan-gua-ges.———— That's

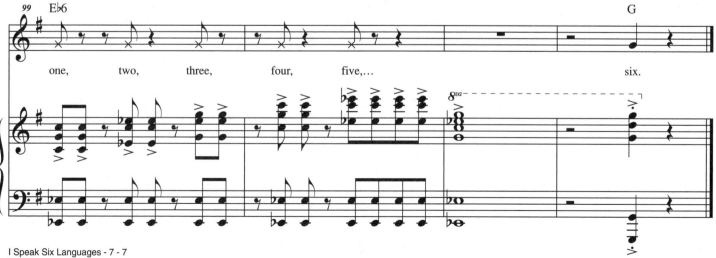

one, two, three, four, five,... six.

I'M NOT AT ALL IN LOVE

(from "The Pajama Game")

Words and Music by
RICHARD ADLER and JERRY ROSS

© 1954 FRANK MUSIC CORP.
Copyright Renewed and Assigned to J & J ROSS CO. and LAKSHMI PUJA MUSIC LTD.
All Rights Administered by THE SONGWRITERS GUILD OF AMERICA
All Rights Reserved

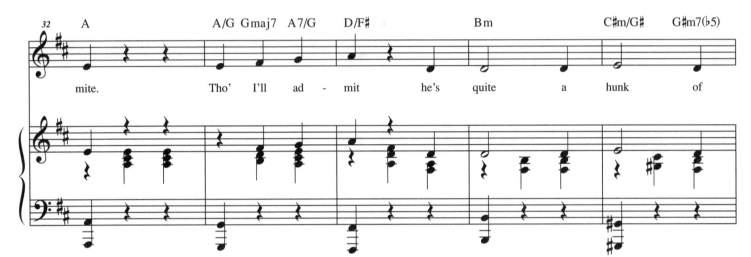

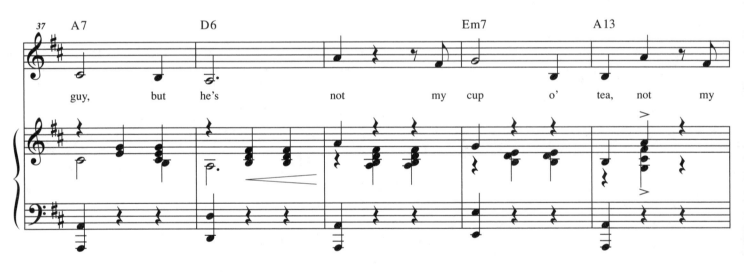

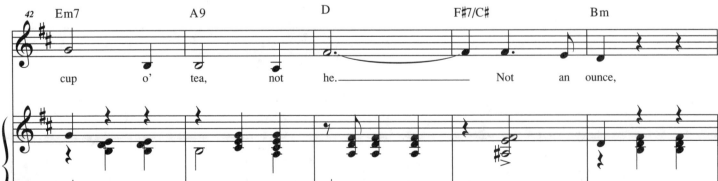

*For solo option, ignore character names.

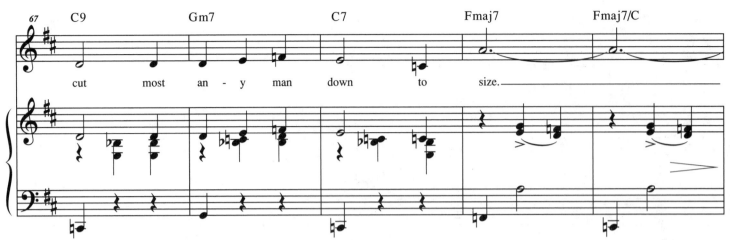

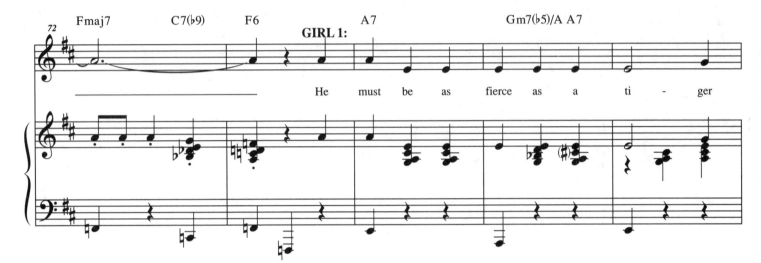

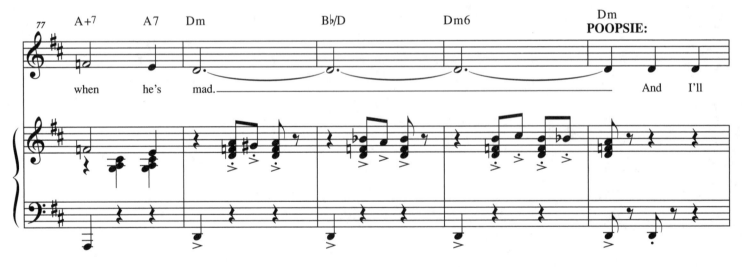

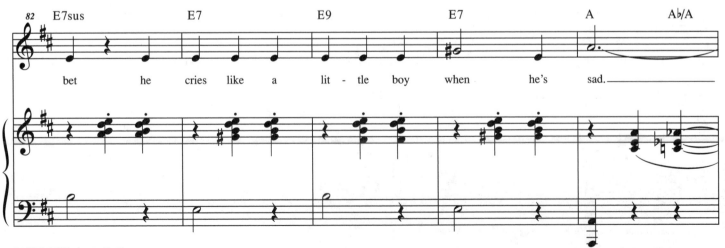

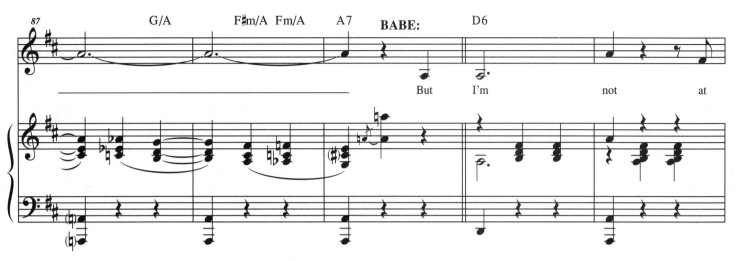

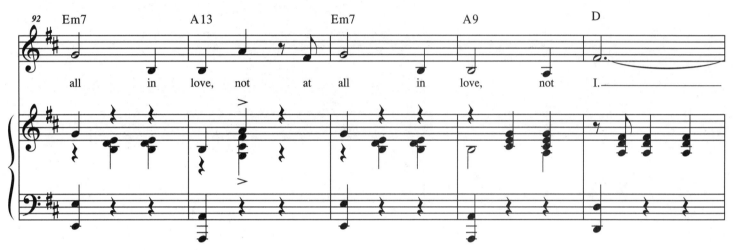

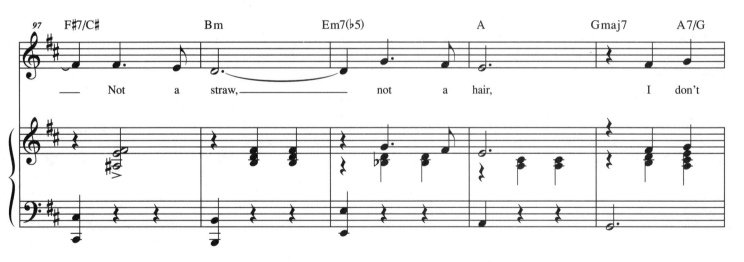

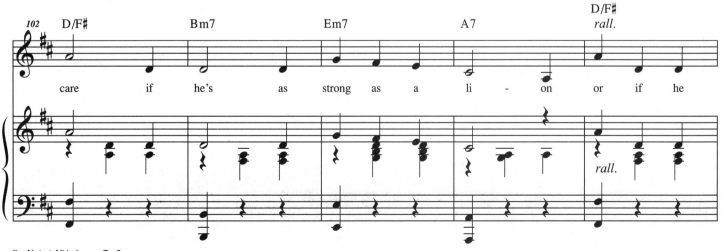

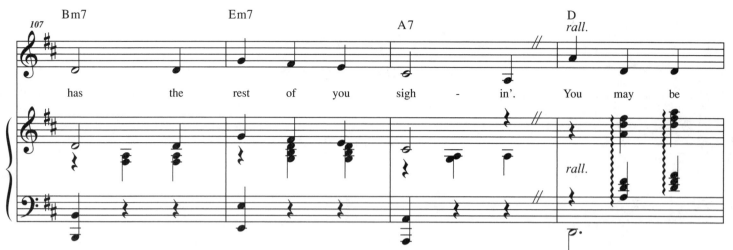

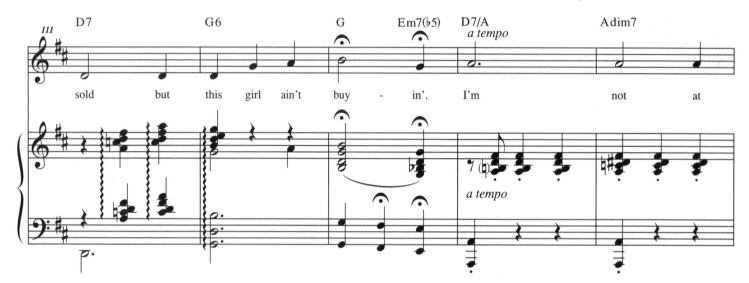

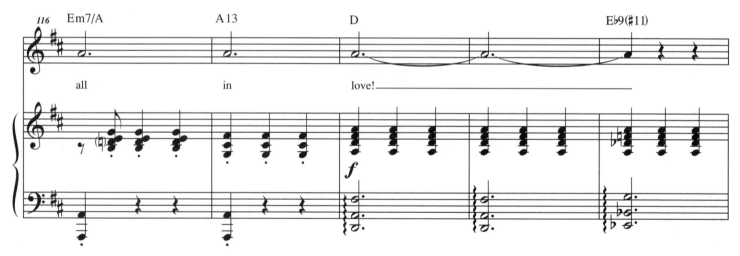

IS IT REALLY ME?

(from "110 in the Shade")

Words by
TOM JONES

Music by
HARVEY SCHMIDT

© 1964 (Renewed) TOM JONES and HARVEY SCHMIDT
Publication and Allied Rights Assigned to CHAPPELL & CO., INC.
All Rights Reserved

see.
Some - one who is beau - ti - ful;
Is it real - ly me?
Mo - ments a - go
I was a - lone
hop - ing that this could be.
Now here I am,
safe in your arms.
And I'm no long - er

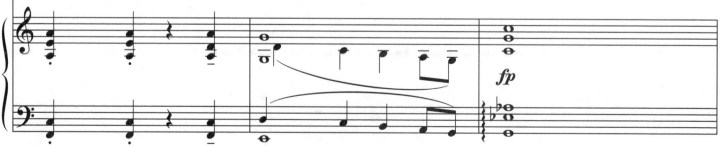

MAMA WHO BORE ME

(from "Spring Awakening")

Lyrics by
STEVEN SATER

Music by
DUNCAN SHEIK

© 2006 KUKUZO MUSIC, UNIVERSAL MUSIC-CAREERS, HAPP-DOG MUSIC and DUNCAN SHEIK SONGS
All Rights For KUKUZO MUSIC Administered by WARNER-TAMERLANE PUBLISHING CORP.
All Rights Reserved

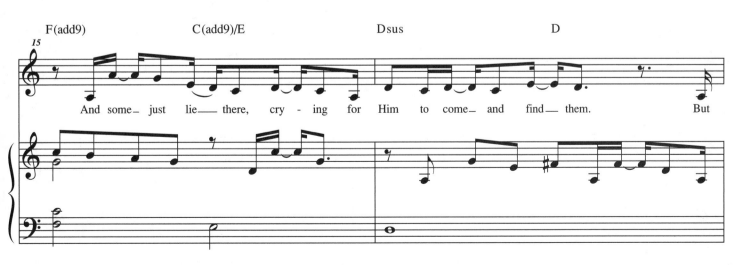

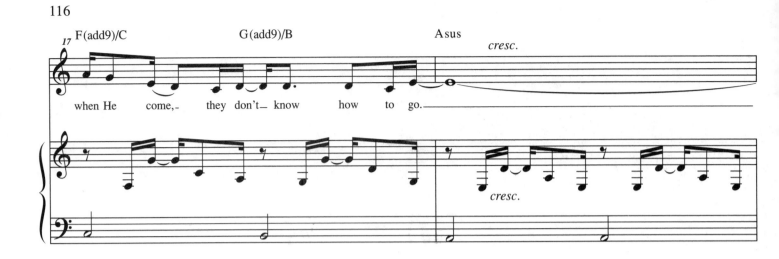

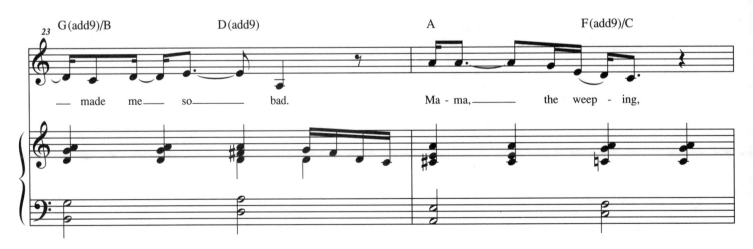

Ma - ma,———— the an - gels. No sleep—— in Heav - en——————

or Beth - le - hem.————

MAMMA MIA
(from "Mamma Mia!")

Words and Music by
BENNY ANDERSSON, STIG ANDERSON
and BJORN ULVAEUS

1. I was cheat-ed by you____ and I think you know when.____
2. I was an-gry and sad____ when I knew we were through.____

So I made up my mind____ it must come to an end.____
I can't count all the times____ I have cried o-ver you.____

© 1975 (Renewed) by UNION SONGS AB (Sweden)
All Rights in the U.S. and Canada Administered by EMI GROVE PARK MUSIC INC.
and UNIVERSAL-SONGS OF POLYGRAM INTERNATIONAL, INC.
Print Rights on Behalf of EMI GROVE PARK MUSIC, INC. Administered by ALFRED PUBLISHING CO., INC.
All Rights Reserved

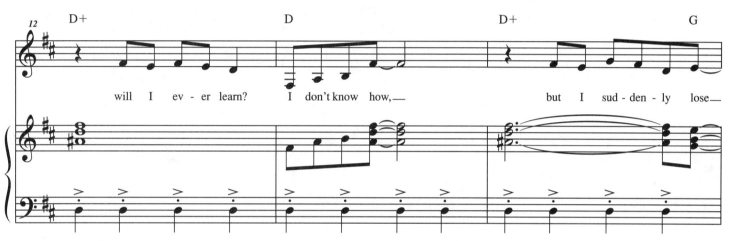

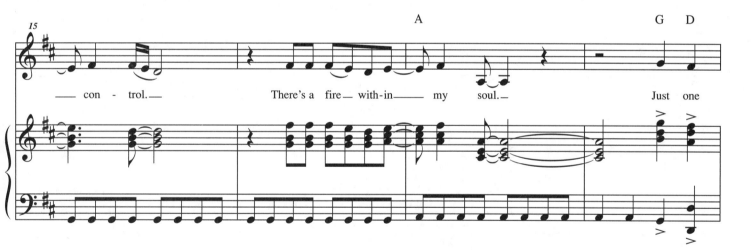

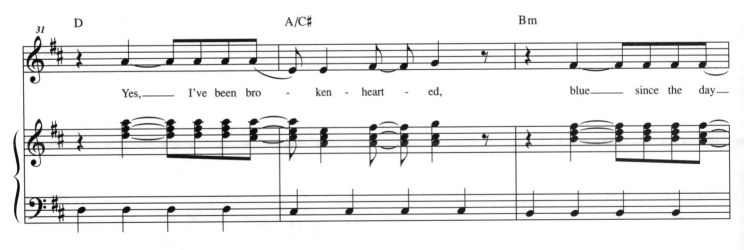

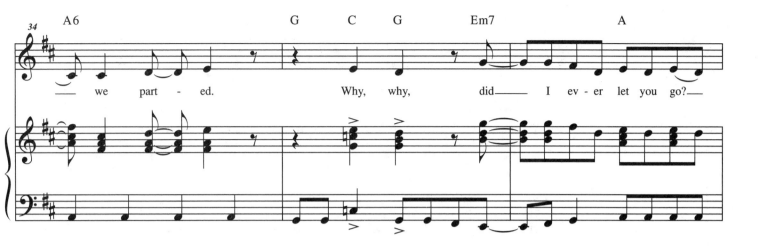

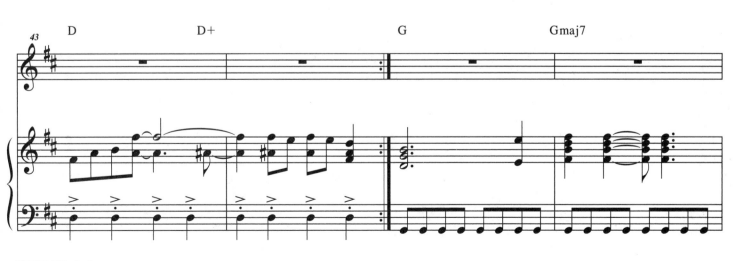

Mamma Mia - 6 - 4
32024

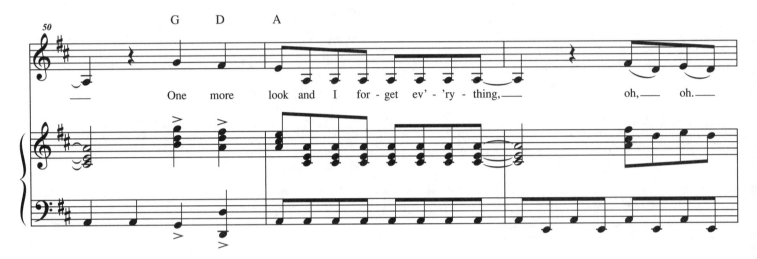

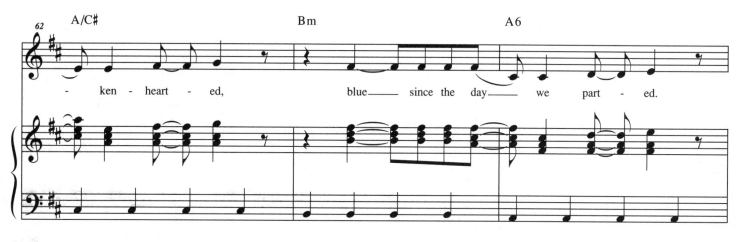

MUCH MORE

(from "The Fantasticks")

Lyrics by
TOM JONES

Music by
HARVEY SCHMIDT

© 1960, 1963 (Copyrights Renewed) TOM JONES and HARVEY SCHMIDT
Publication and Allied Rights Assigned to CHAPPELL & CO., INC.
All Rights Reserved

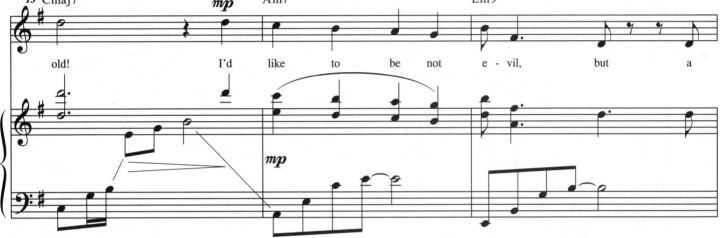

Same tempo — non accel.

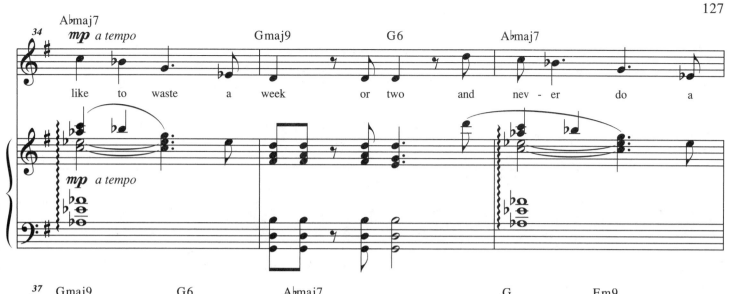

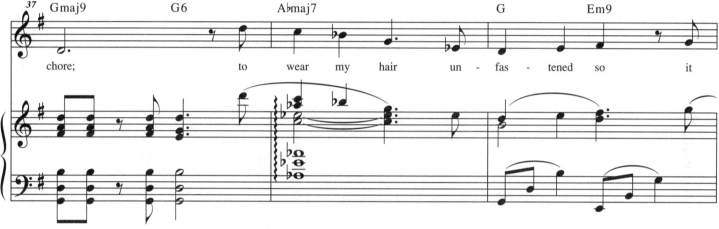

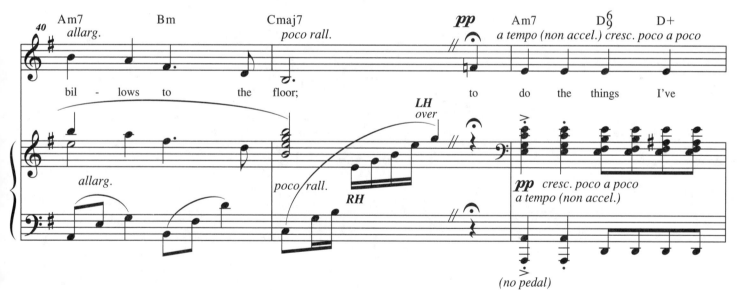

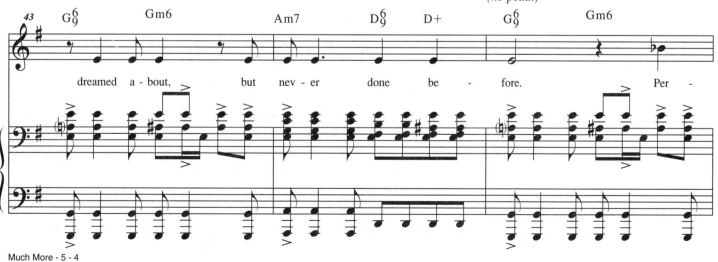

THE MUSIC THAT MAKES ME DANCE

(from "Funny Girl")

Lyrics by
BOB MERRILL

Music by
JULE STYNE

The Music That Makes Me Dance - 4 - 1
32024

© 1964 (Renewed) by BOB MERRILL and JULE STYNE
Publication and Allied Rights Assigned to WONDERFUL MUSIC, INC. and Administered by CHAPPELL & CO., INC.
All Rights Reserved

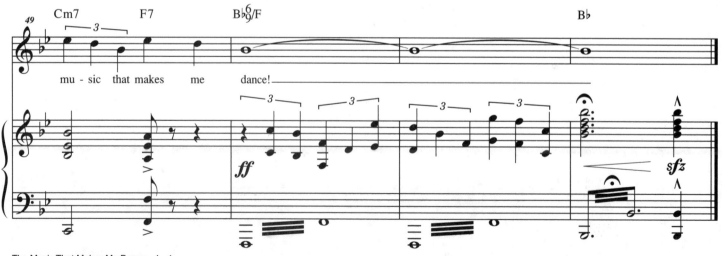

THE NEW GIRL IN TOWN

(from "Hairspray")

Lyrics by
SCOTT WITTMAN and
MARC SHAIMAN

Music by
MARC SHAIMAN

The New Girl in Town - 8 - 1
32024

© 2007 NEW LINE TUNES
All Rights Reserved

af - ter school!___ And yet,___ we'd like to be like her,___ 'cause

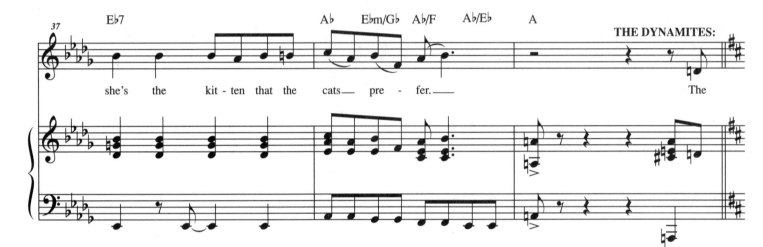

she's the kit - ten that the cats___ pre - fer.___ The

THE DYNAMITES:

new girl in town___ has my guy on a string.___ The

new girl in town,___ *hey, look, she's wear - ing his ring!*___

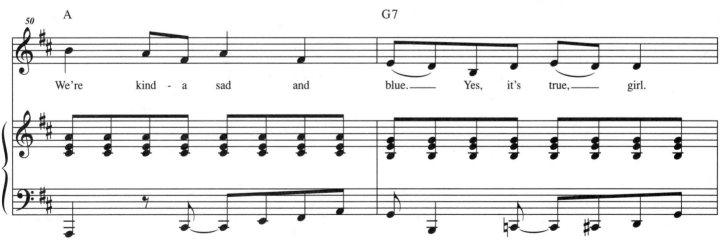

Double-time gospel feel

PART OF YOUR WORLD

(from Walt Disney's "The Little Mermaid")

Lyrics by
HOWARD ASHMAN

Music by
ALAN MENKEN

(with pedal)

© 1988 WALT DISNEY MUSIC COMPANY and WONDERLAND MUSIC COMPANY, INC.
All Rights Reserved   Used by Permission

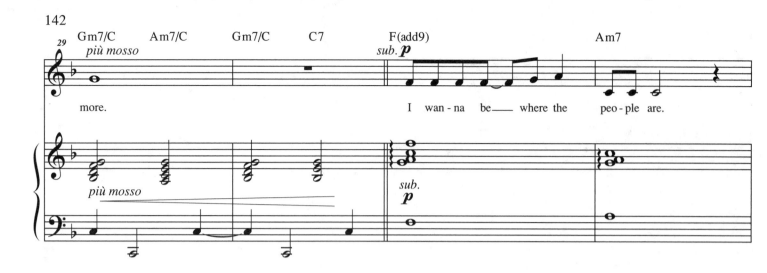

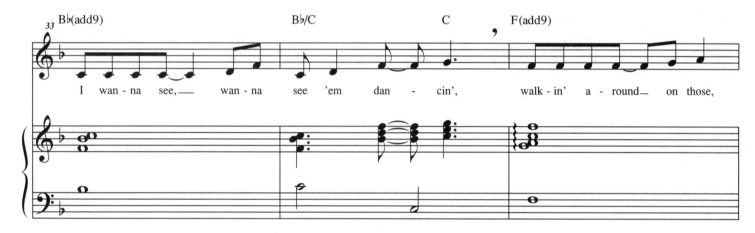

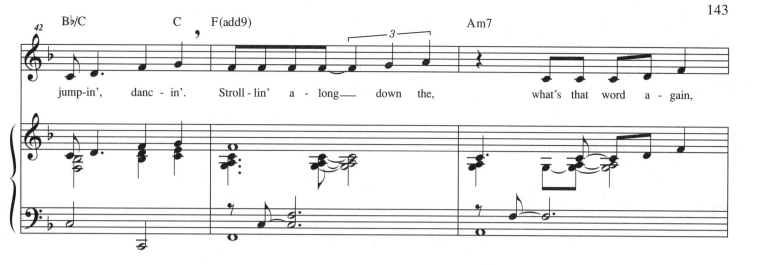

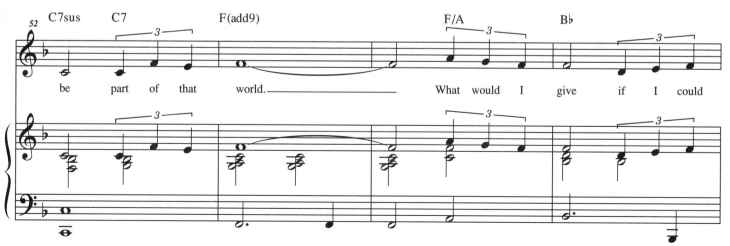

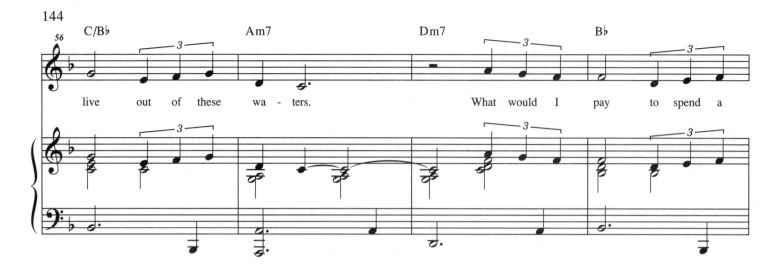

live out of these wa - ters. What would I pay to spend a

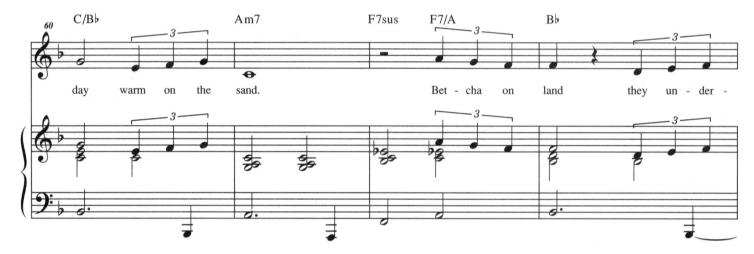

day warm on the sand. Bet - cha on land they un - der -

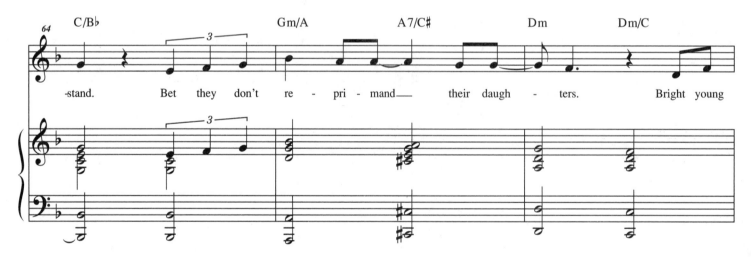

-stand. Bet they don't re - pri - mand___ their daugh - ters. Bright young

wo - men, sick of swim - min', read - y to stand.___ And

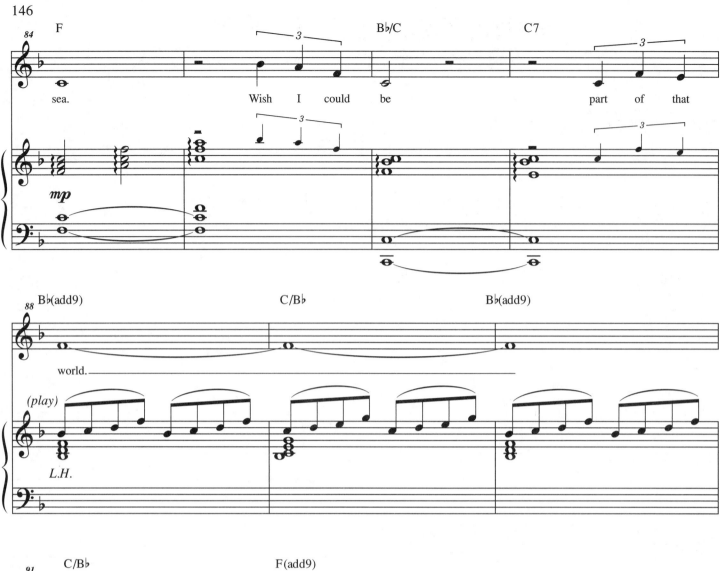

sea.   Wish I could be   part of that

world.

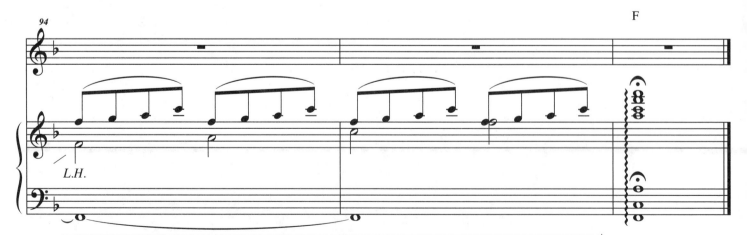

PRACTICALLY PERFECT

(from "Mary Poppins: The New Musical")

Lyrics by
ANTHONY DREWE

Music by
GEORGE STILES

CD 2
Track 6

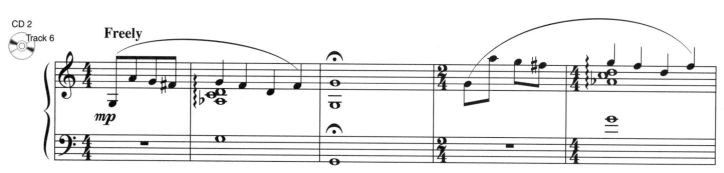

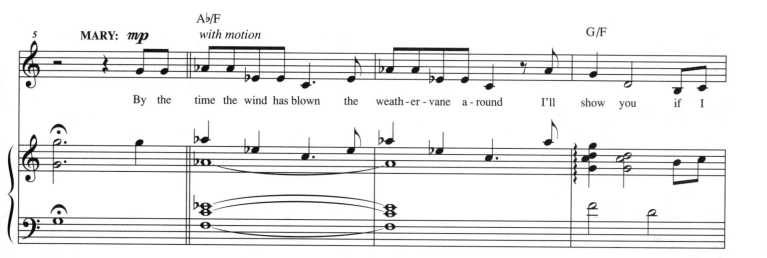

© 2005 WONDERLAND MUSIC COMPANY, INC. and CAMERON MACKINTOSH LTD.
All Rights Administered by WONDERLAND MUSIC COMPANY, INC.
All Rights Reserved   Used by Permission

In 2 (♩ = 90)

char - ac - ter   is   spit, spot, spick and   span.   I'm prac - ti - cal - ly   per - fect_____

_____ in   ev - 'ry   way.   Prac - ti - cal - ly   per - fect

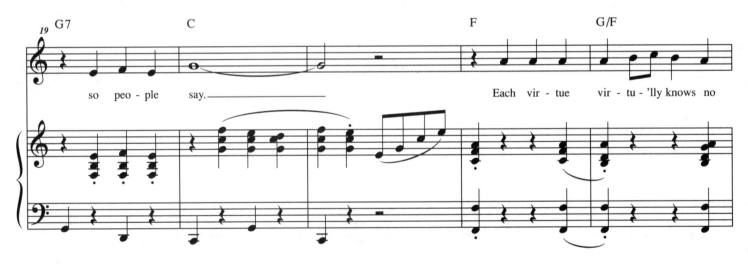

so   peo - ple   say._____   Each vir - tue   vir - tu - 'lly knows no

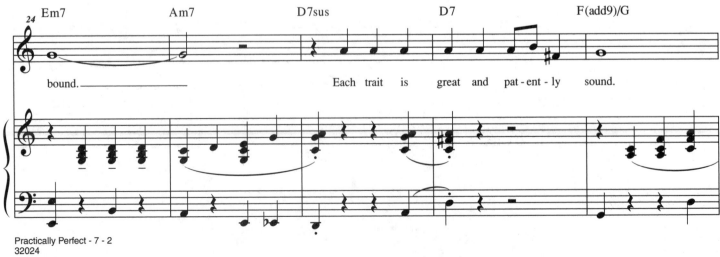

bound._____   Each trait is   great and pat - ent - ly   sound.

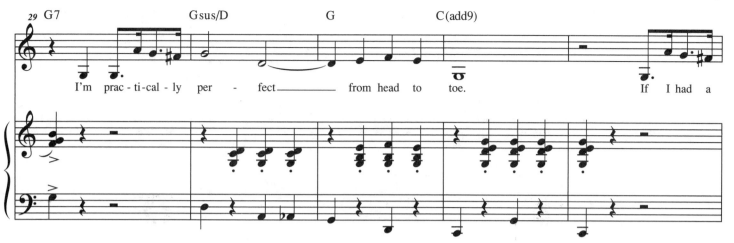

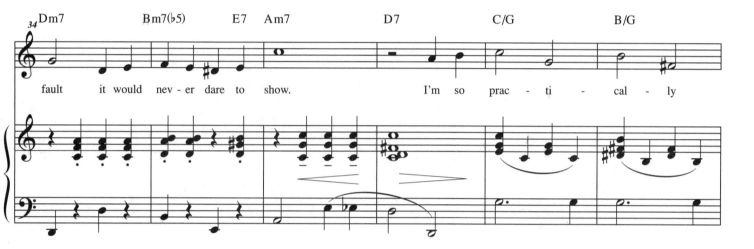

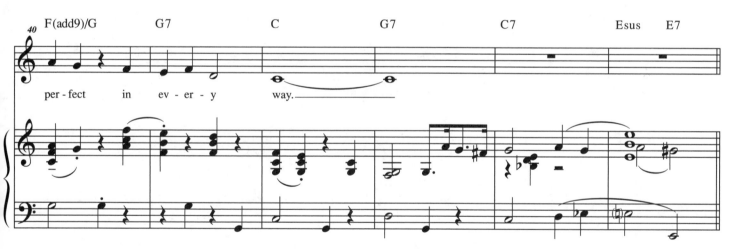

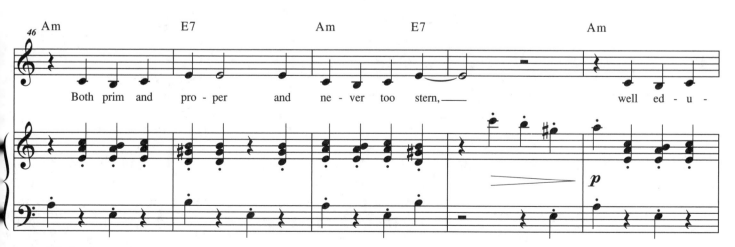

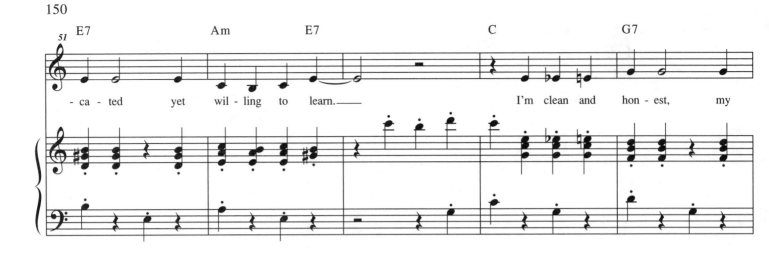

-ca- ted yet wil- ling to learn.___ I'm clean and hon- est, my

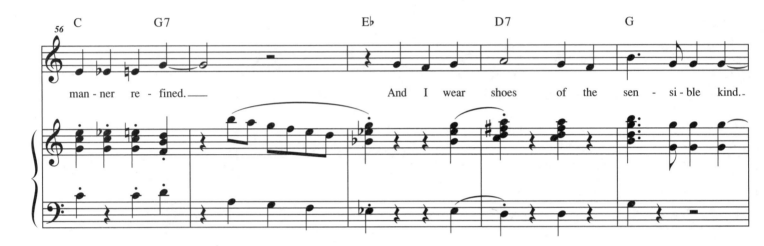

man- ner re- fined.___ And I wear shoes of the sen- si- ble kind.___

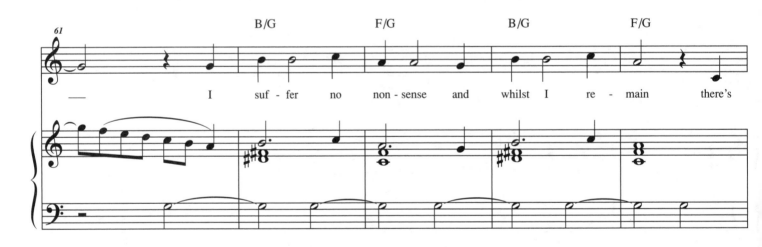

___ I suf- fer no non- sense and whilst I re- main there's

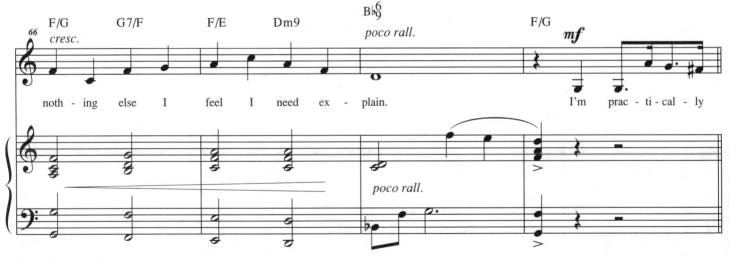

noth- ing else I feel I need ex- plain. I'm prac- ti- cal- ly

Slightly quicker (♩ = 100)

per - fect_____ in ev - 'ry way. Prac - ti-cal - ly per - fect,

that's my for - te._____ Un - can - ny nan - nies are hard to

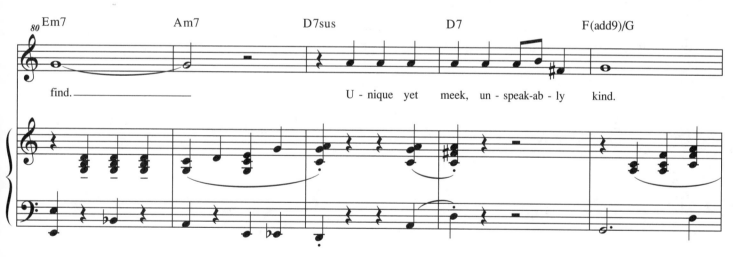

find._____ U - nique yet meek, un - speak-ab - ly kind.

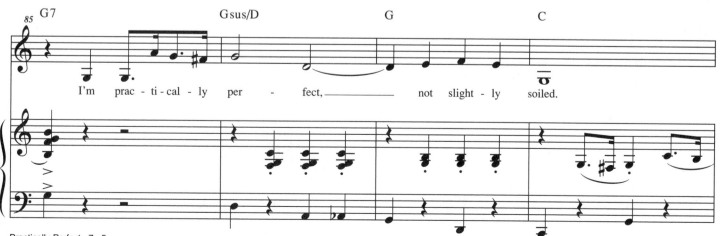

I'm prac - ti-cal - ly per - fect,_____ not slight - ly soiled.

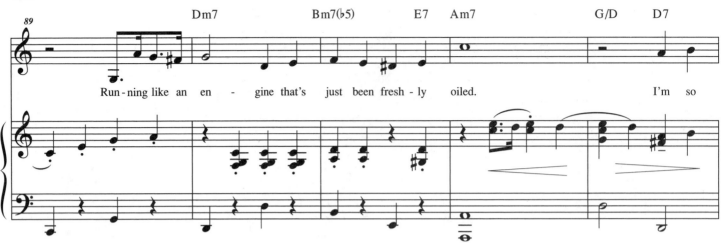

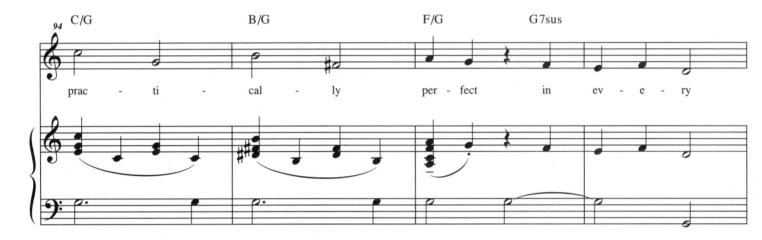

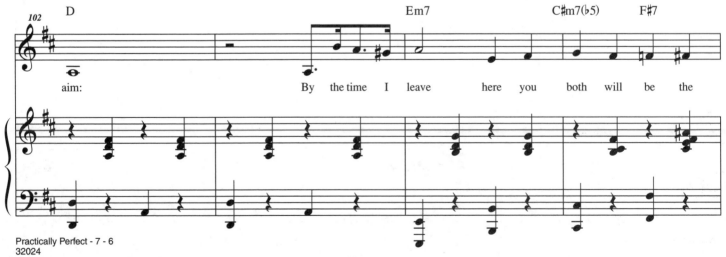

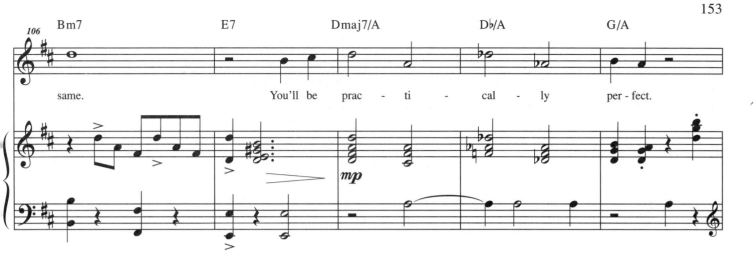

same. You'll be prac - ti - cal - ly per - fect.

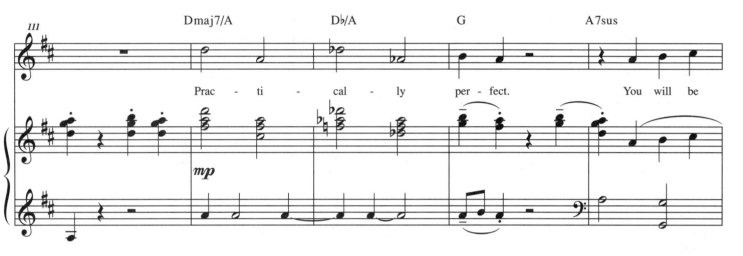

Prac - ti - cal - ly per - fect. You will be

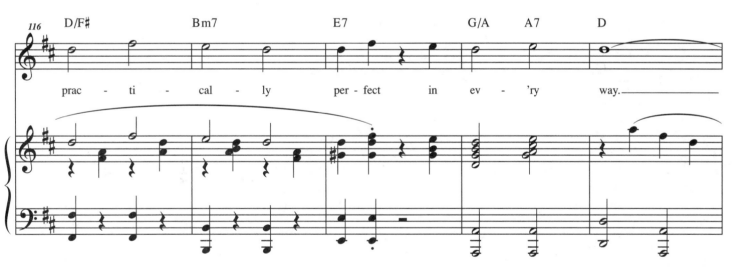

prac - ti - cal - ly per - fect in ev - 'ry way.

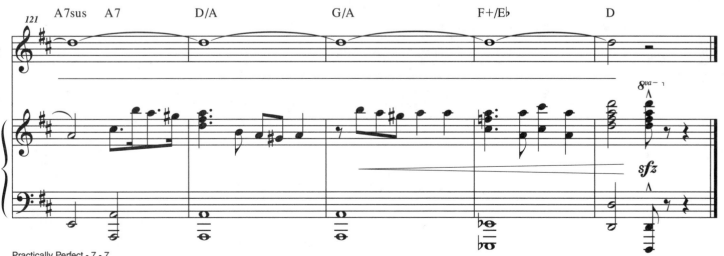

PRINCESS
(from "A Man of No Importance")

Lyrics by
LYNN AHRENS

Music by
STEPHEN FLAHERTY

© 2002 WB MUSIC CORP., PEN AND PERSERVERANCE and HILLSDALE MUSIC, INC.
All Rights Administered by WB MUSIC CORP.
All Rights Reserved

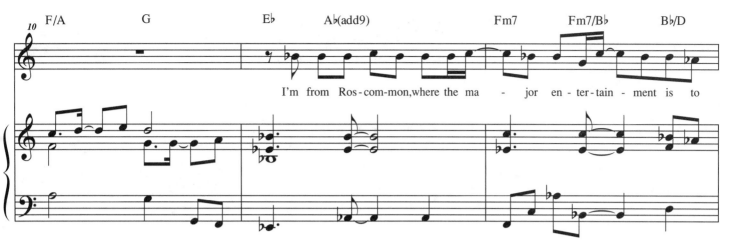

I'm from Ros-com-mon, where the ma - jor en-ter-tain-ment is to

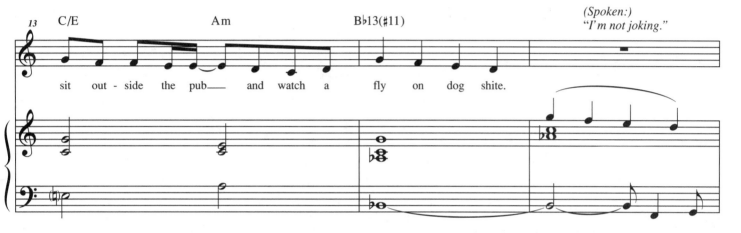

(Spoken:)
"I'm not joking."

sit out-side the pub___ and watch a fly on dog shite.

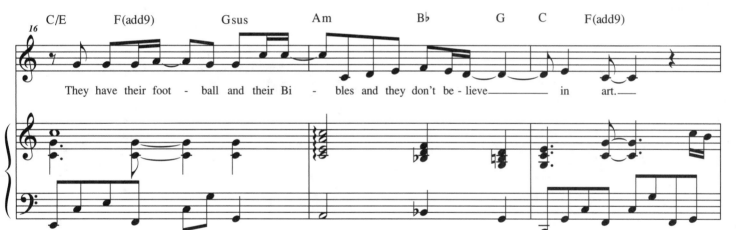

They have their foot - ball and their Bi - bles and they don't be-lieve___ in art.___

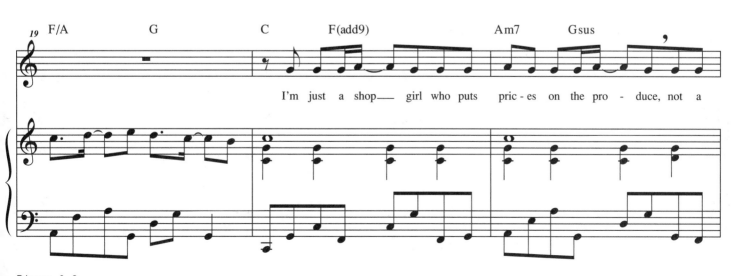

I'm just a shop___ girl who puts pric - es on the pro - duce, not a

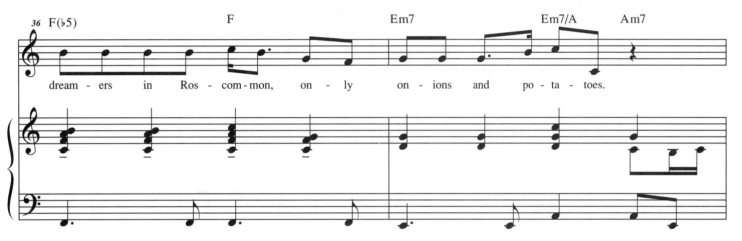

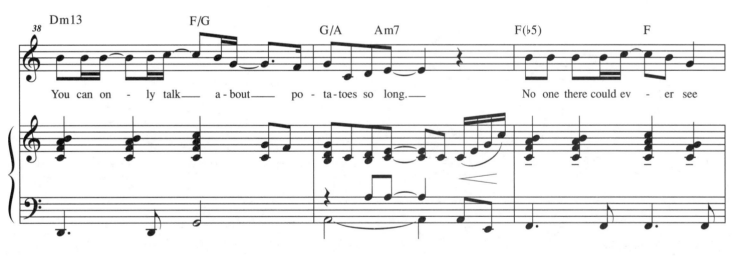

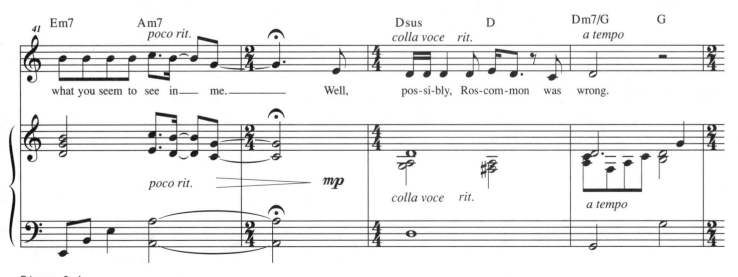

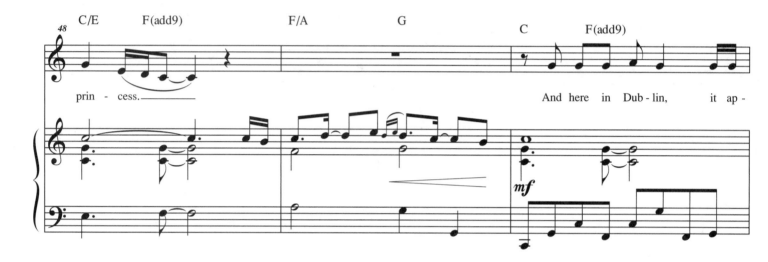

RAUNCHY
(from "110 in the Shade")

Words by
TOM JONES

Music by
HARVEY SCHMIDT

© 1964 (Renewed) TOM JONES and HARVEY SCHMIDT
Publication and Allied Rights Assigned to CHAPPELL & CO., INC.
All Rights Reserved

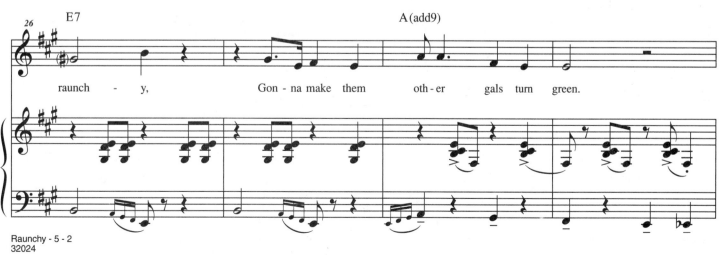

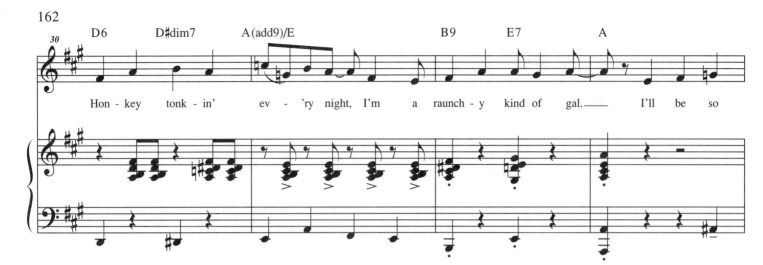

Hon-key tonk-in' ev-'ry night, I'm a raunch-y kind of gal.___ I'll be so

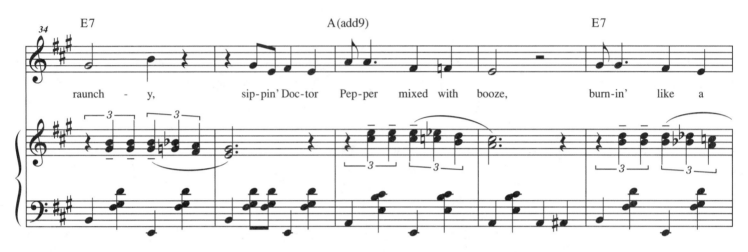

raunch - y, sip-pin' Doc-tor Pep-per mixed with booze, burn-in' like a

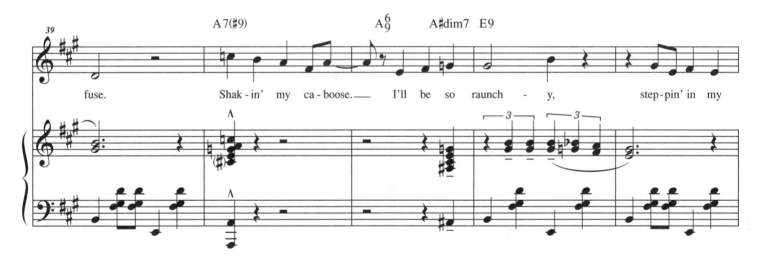

fuse. Shak-in' my ca-boose.___ I'll be so raunch - y, step-pin' in my

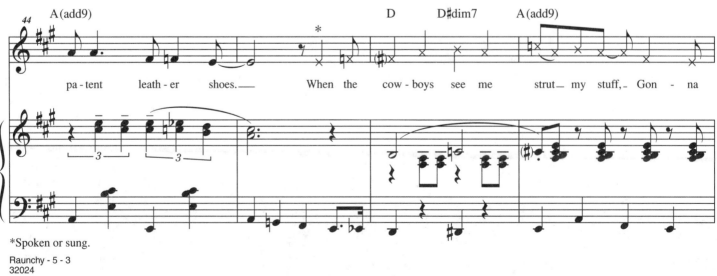

pa-tent leath-er shoes.___ When the cow-boys see me strut— my stuff,— Gon - na

*Spoken or sung.

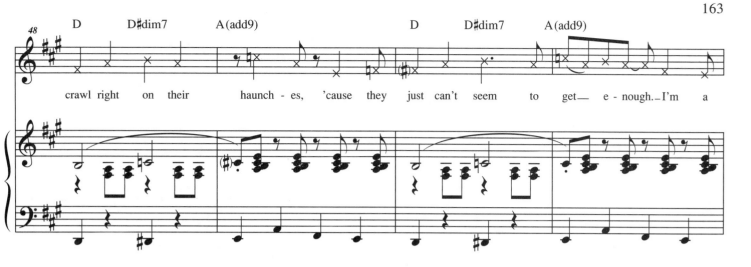

crawl right on their haunch - es, 'cause they just can't seem to get— e - nough.—I'm a

L'istesso tempo; Quick Honkey-Tonk

raunch - y kind of gal.— I'll be so raunch - y, When I'm danc-in' up and down the

street, of the coun - ty seat.— Tip - py tap-pin' feet.— I'll be so

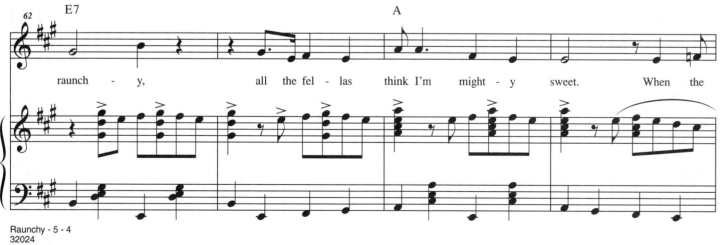

raunch - y, all the fel - las think I'm might - y sweet. When the

Stripper tempo

ROXIE

(from "Chicago")

Lyrics by
FRED EBB

Music by
JOHN KANDER

CD 2
Track 9

© 1975 (Renewed) KANDER & EBB INC. and UNICHAPPELL MUSIC INC.
All Rights Administered by UNICHAPPELL MUSIC INC.
All Rights Reserved

Roxie - 8 - 1
32024

somebody ev'ryone knows. They're gonna recognize my eyes, my

hair, my teeth, my boobs, my nose.

From just some dumb mechanic's wife I'm gonna be Roxie.

Who says that murder's not an art? And

*Performance option for group verses solo. Use secondary lyrics.

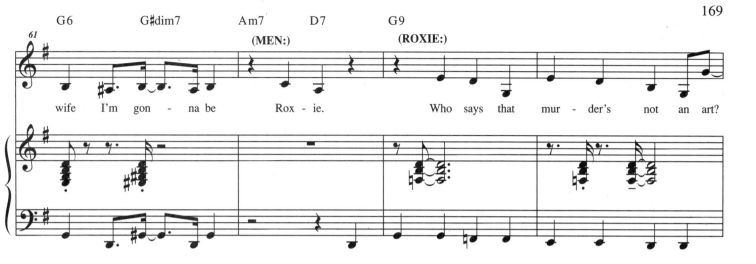

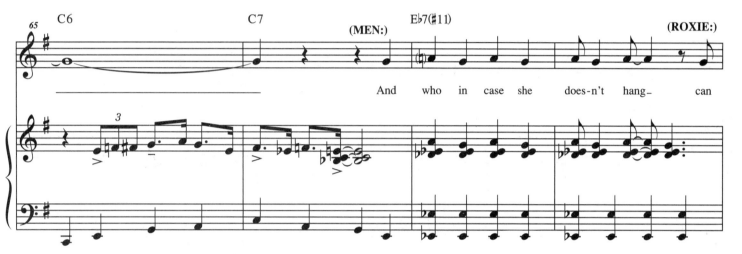

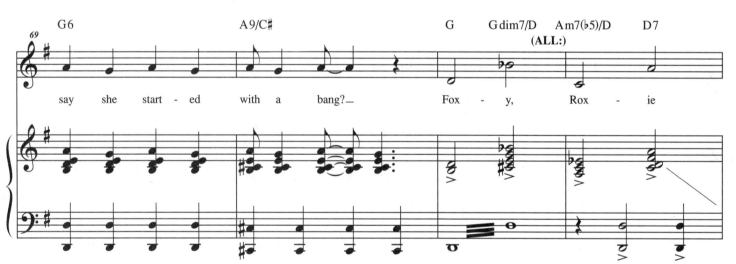

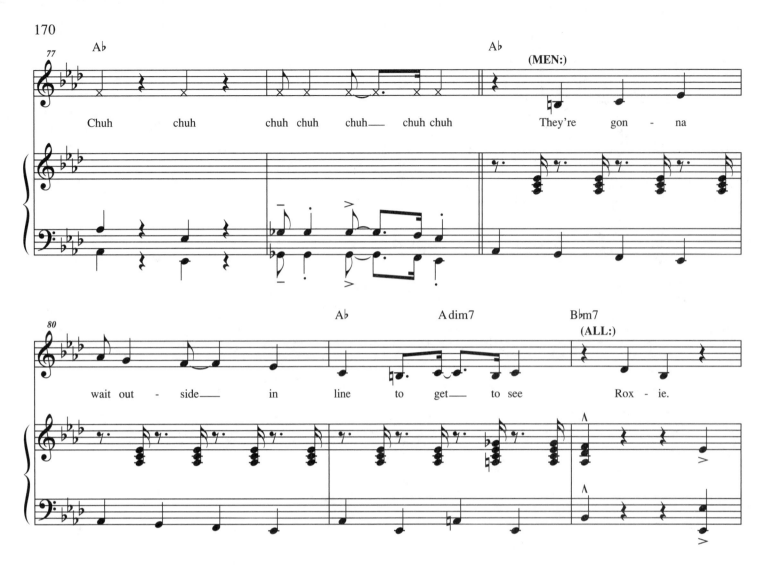

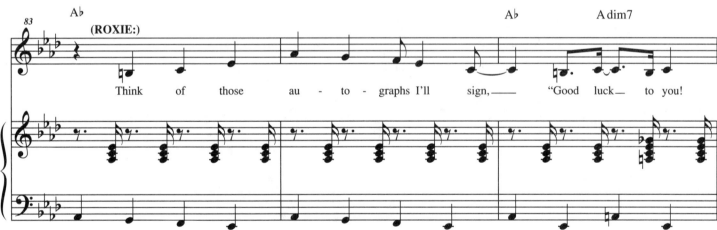

So - phie Tuck - er-'ll shit I know___ to see her name get

billed be - low___ Fox - y, Rox - ie Hart! Chuh

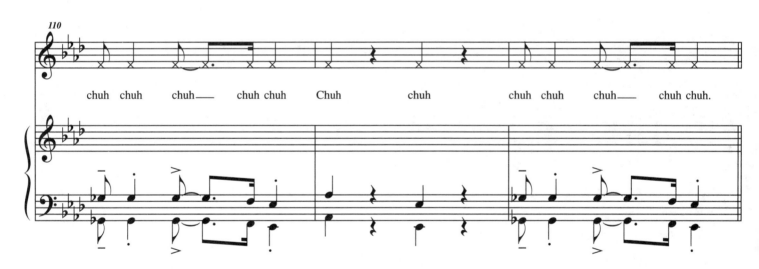

chuh chuh chuh___ chuh chuh Chuh chuh chuh chuh chuh___ chuh chuh.

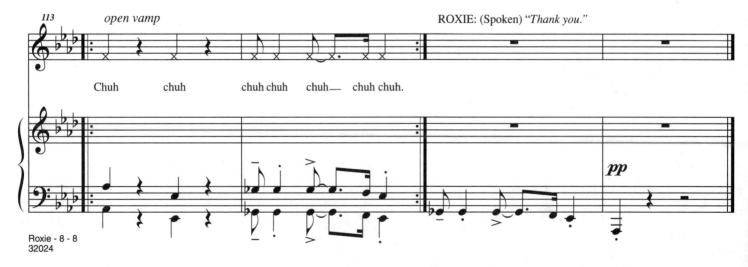

Chuh chuh chuh chuh chuh___ chuh chuh.

SHOW ME

(from "My Fair Lady")

Words by
ALAN JAY LERNER

Music by
FREDERICK LOEWE

© 1956 (Renewed) by ALAN JAY LERNER and FREDERICK LOEWE
Publication and Allied Rights Assigned to CHAPPELL & CO., INC.
All Rights Reserved

Show Me - 5 - 1
32024

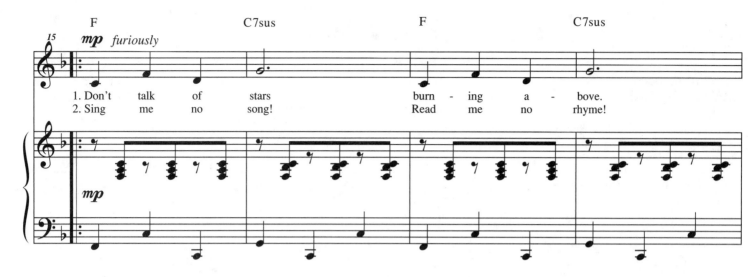

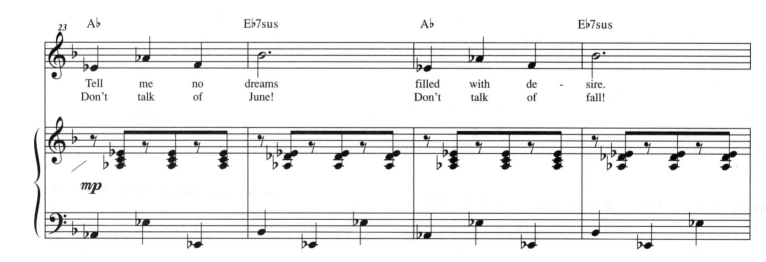

*Pronounced "expl'ine."

SHY
(from "Once Upon a Mattress")

Words by
MARSHALL BARER

Music by
MARY RODGERS

© 1959 (Renewed) CHAPPELL & CO., INC.
All Rights Reserved

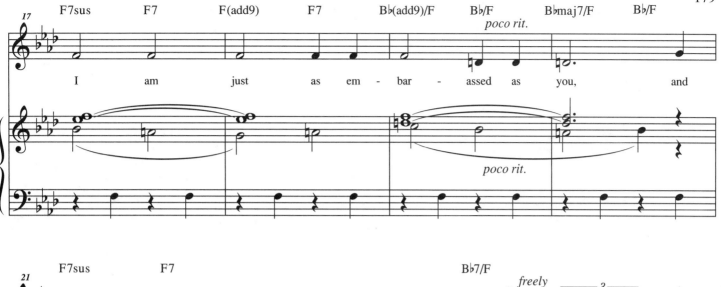

F7sus F7 F(add9) F7 B♭(add9)/F B♭/F B♭maj7/F B♭/F

poco rit.

I am just as em - bar - assed as you, and

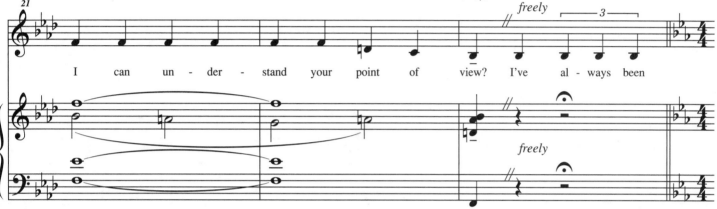

F7sus F7 B♭7/F

freely

I can un - der - stand your point of view? I've al - ways been

Moderate swing (♩ = 160)

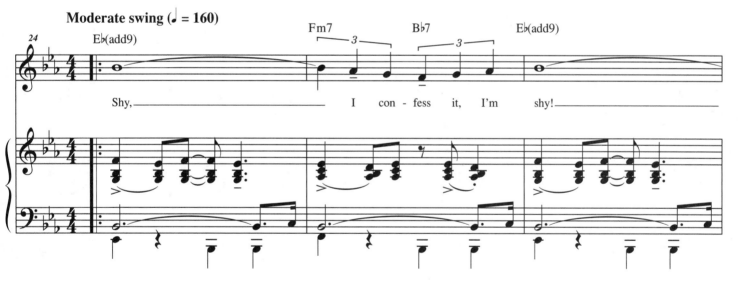

E♭(add9) Fm7 B♭7 E♭(add9)

Shy,_____ I con - fess it, I'm shy!_____

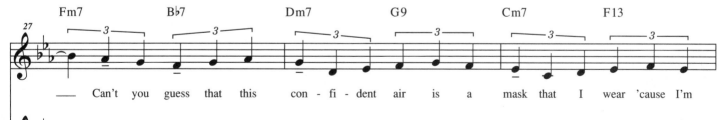

Fm7 B♭7 Dm7 G9 Cm7 F13

— Can't you guess that this con - fi - dent air is a mask that I wear 'cause I'm

Shy - 5 - 2
32024

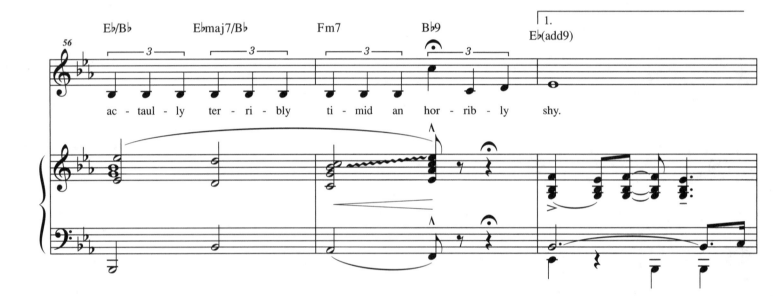

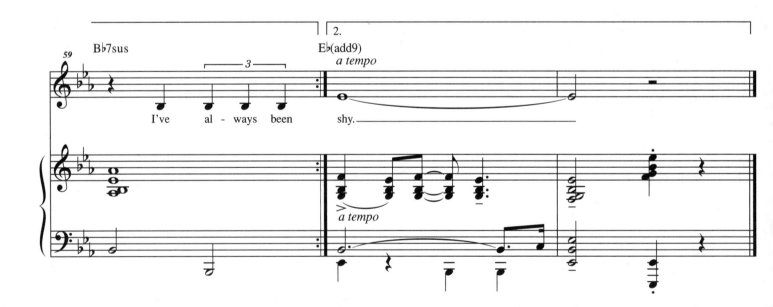

THE SIMPLE JOYS OF MAIDENHOOD

(from "Camelot")

Lyrics by
ALAN JAY LERNER

Music by
FREDERICK LOEWE

© 1960 (Renewed) by ALAN JAY LERNER and FREDERICK LOEWE
Publication and Allied Rights Assigned to CHAPPELL & CO., INC.
ALL RIGHTS RESERVED

The Simple Joys of Maidenhood - 4 - 2
32024

SOMEWHERE THAT'S GREEN

(from "Little Shop of Horrors")

Lyrics by
HOWARD ASHMAN

Music by
ALAN MENKEN

I know Sey-mour's the great-est but I'm da-ting a se-mi-sa-dist, so I got a black eye and my arm's in a cast. Still that Sey-mour's a cut-ie, well if not, he's got in-ner beau-ty and I

© 1982 TRUNKSONG MUSIC, LTD., MENKEN MUSIC and UNIVERSAL-GEFFEN MUSIC
All Rights Reserved

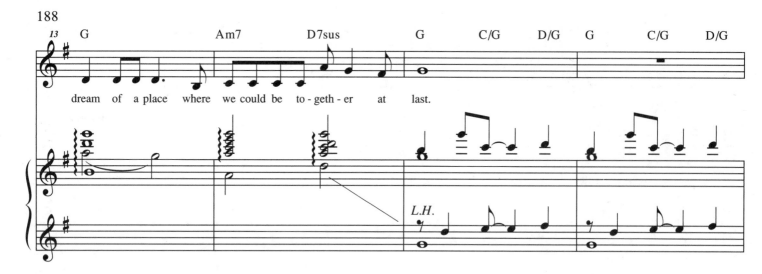

dream of a place where we could be to - geth - er at last.

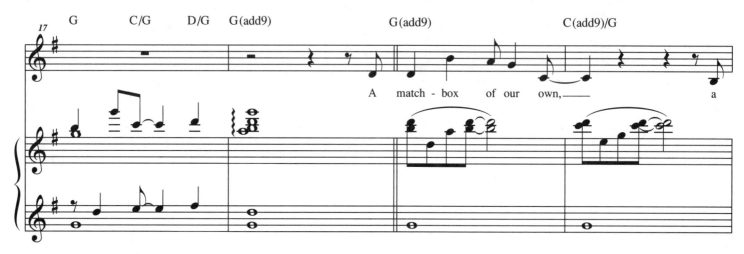

A match - box of our own, _____ a

fence of real chain link, a grill out on the pa - ti - o, _____ dis -

pos - al in the sink, _____ a wash - er and a dry - er and an

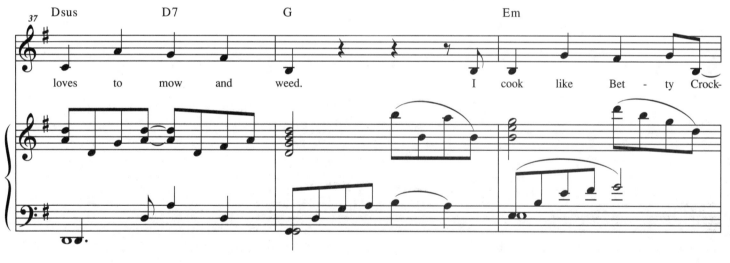

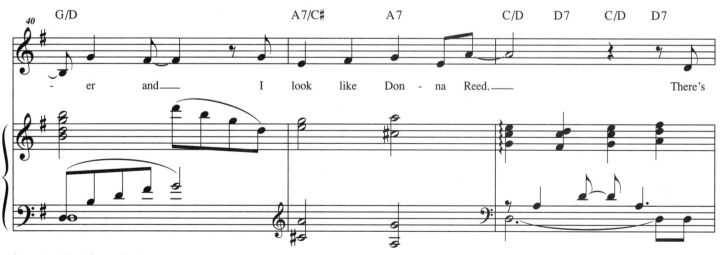

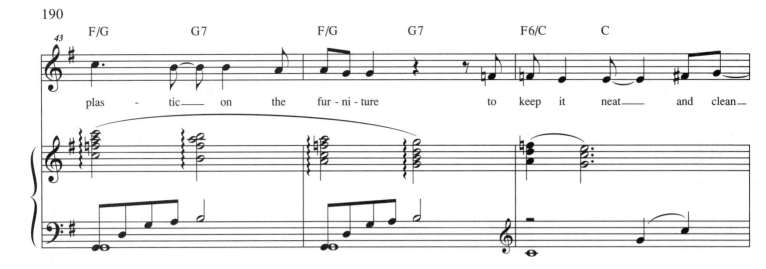

plas - tic___ on the fur - ni - ture to keep it neat___ and clean___

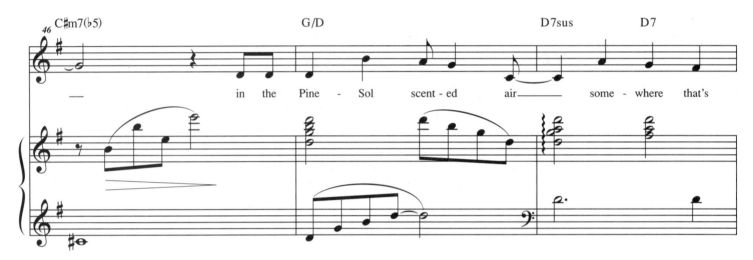

___ in the Pine - Sol scent - ed air___ some - where that's

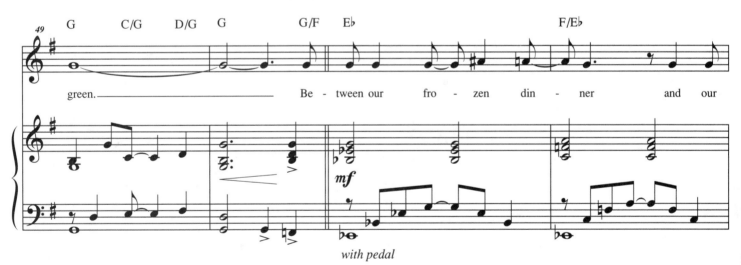

green._____ Be - tween our fro - zen din - ner and our

bed - time, nine fif - teen,___ we snug - gle watch - in' Lu -

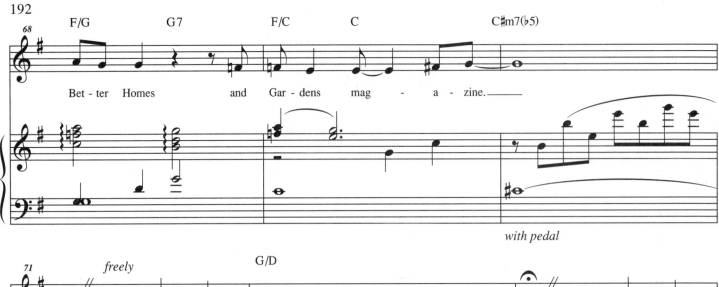

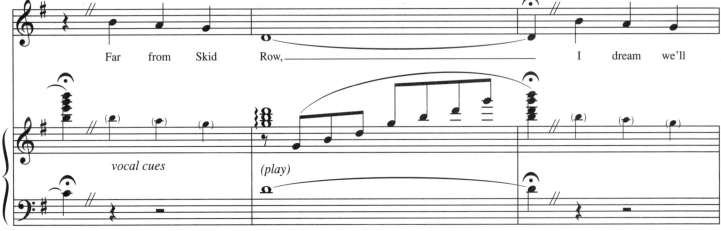

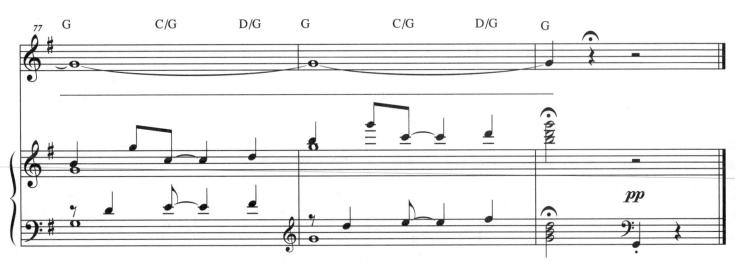

WAITING FOR LIFE

(from "Once on This Island")

Lyrics by
LYNN AHRENS

Music by
STEPHEN FLAHERTY

CD 2
Track 14

Bright Caribbean feel

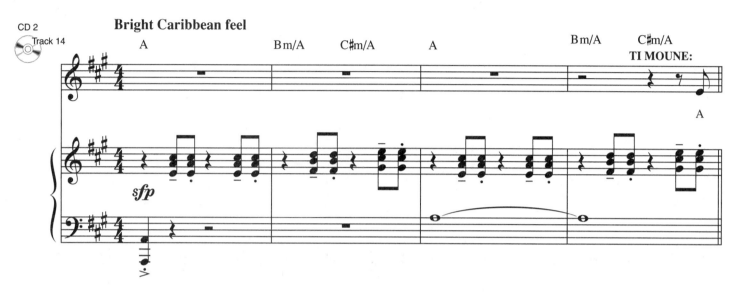

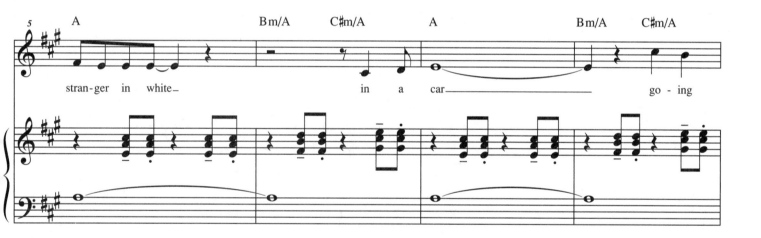

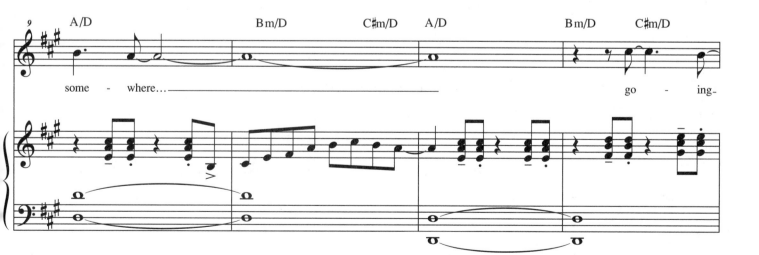

© 1991 WB MUSIC CORP., PEN AND PERSEVERANCE and HILLSDALE MUSIC, INC.
All Rights Administered by WB MUSIC CORP.
All Rights Reserved

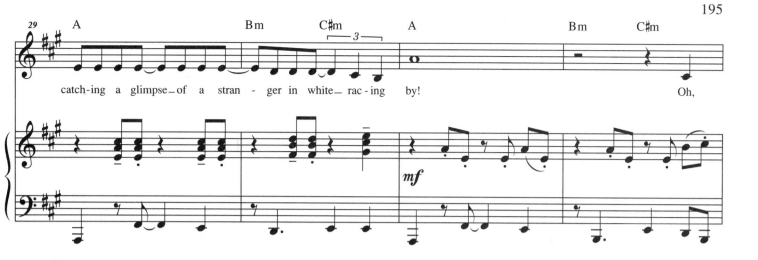

catch-ing a glimpse of a stran - ger in white rac-ing by! Oh,

gods! Oh, gods, are you there?

What can I do to get you to look down and give in? Oh,

gods! Oh, gods, hear my prayer. I'm

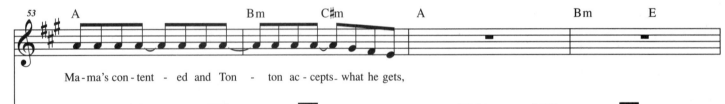

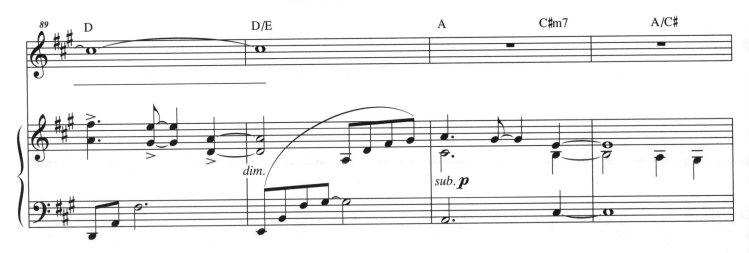

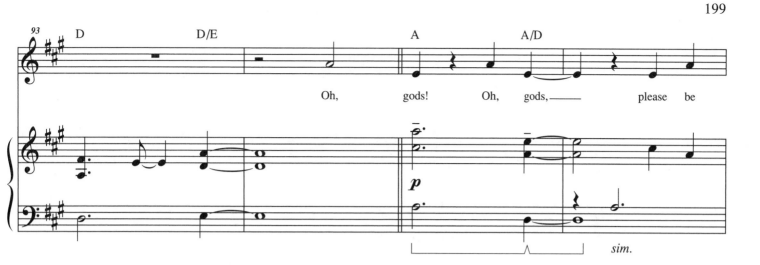

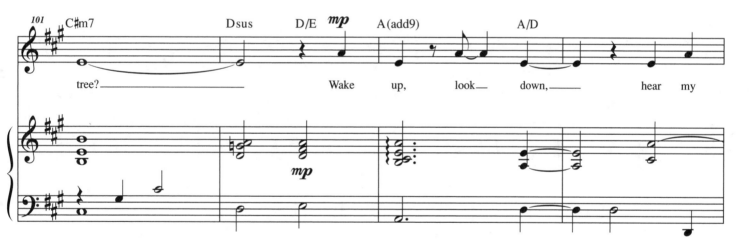

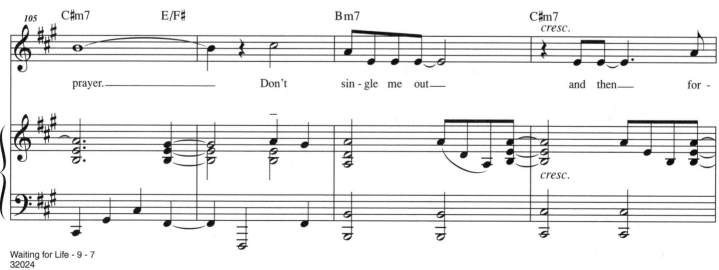

WHISPERING
(from "Spring Awakening")

Lyrics by
STEVEN SATER

Music by
DUNCAN SHEIK

© 2006 KUKUZO MUSIC, UNIVERSAL MUSIC-CAREERS, HAPP-DOG MUSIC and DUNCAN SHEIK SONGS
All Rights For KUKUZO MUSIC Administered by WARNER-TAMERLANE PUBLISHING CORP.
All Rights Reserved

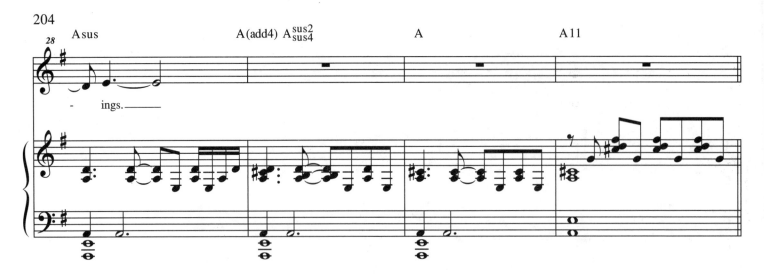

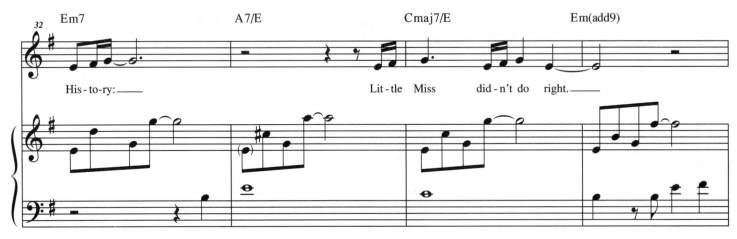

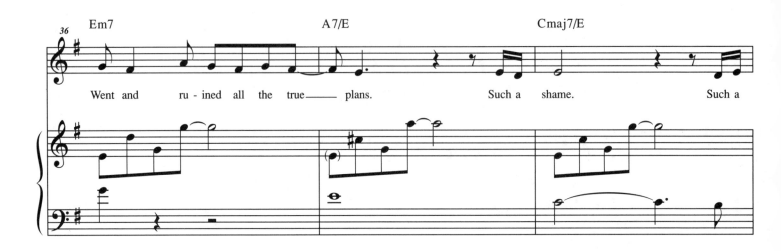

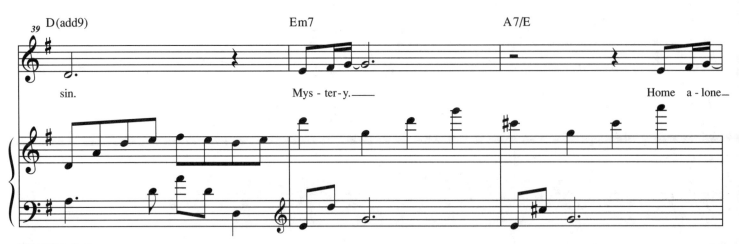

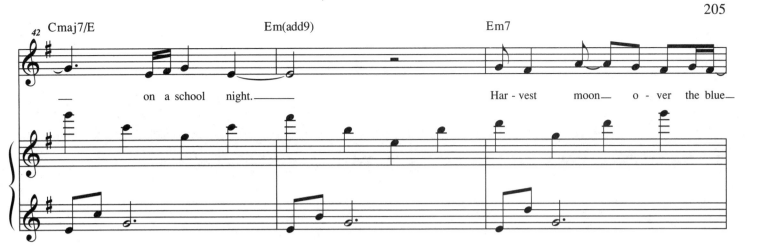

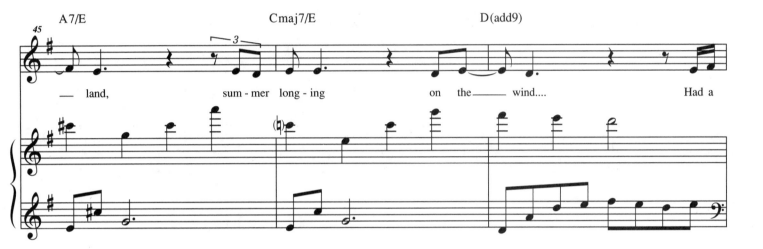

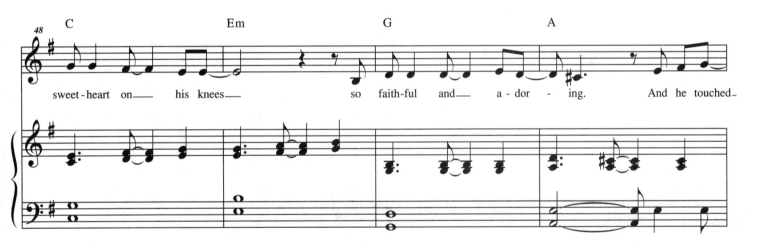

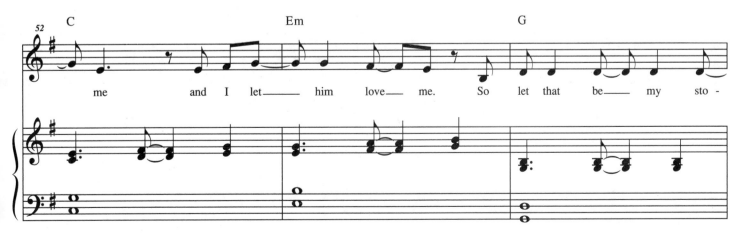

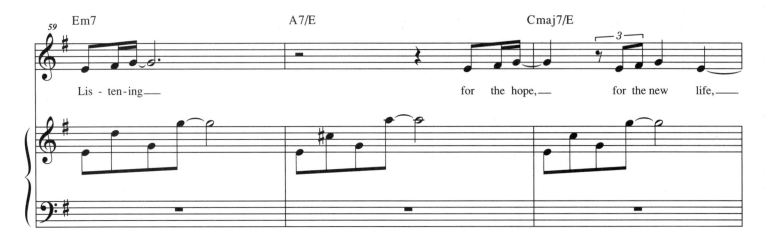

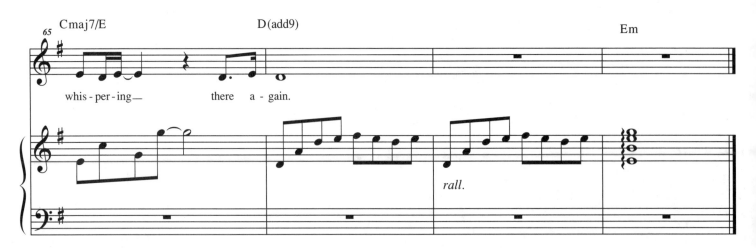

YOUR DADDY'S SON
(from "Ragtime")

Lyrics by
LYNN AHRENS

Music by
STEPHEN FLAHERTY

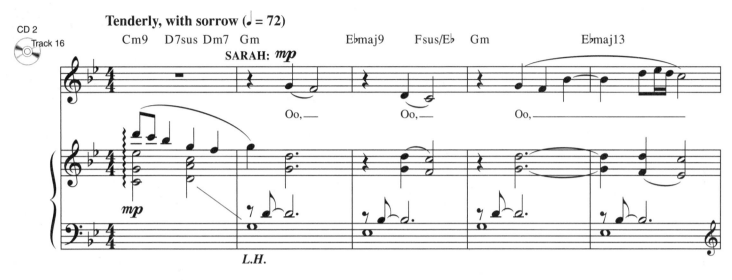

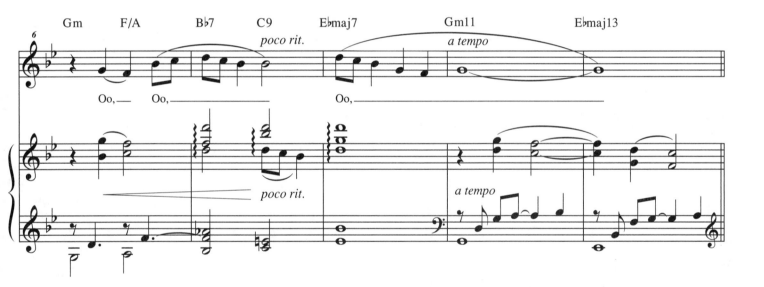

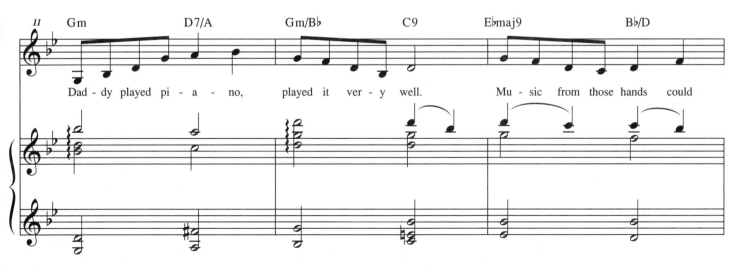

© 1996 WB MUSIC CORP., PEN AND PERSEVERANCE and HILLSDALE MUSIC, INC.
All Rights Administered by WB MUSIC CORP.
All Rights Reserved

208

Your Daddy's Son - 6 - 2
32024

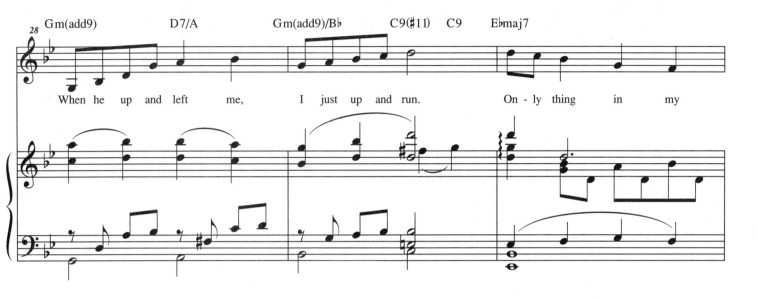

When he up and left me, I just up and run. On - ly thing in my

head, You were your Dad - dy's son.

poco rit.

f più mosso

(with pedal) - - - - - - - - - - - - - - - - - -

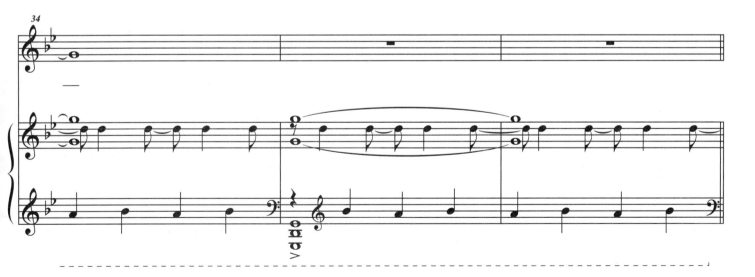

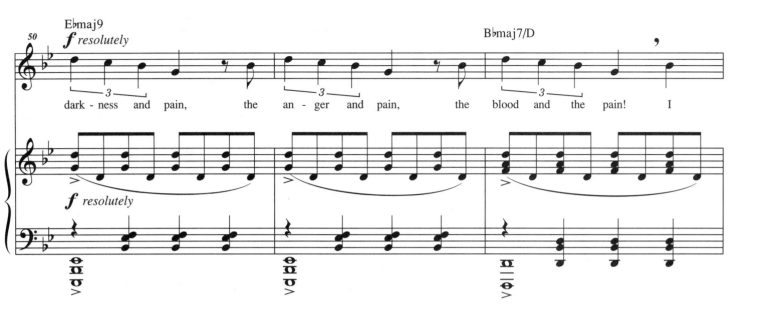

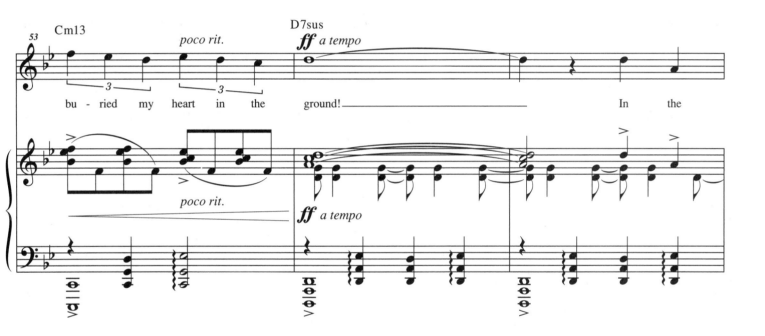

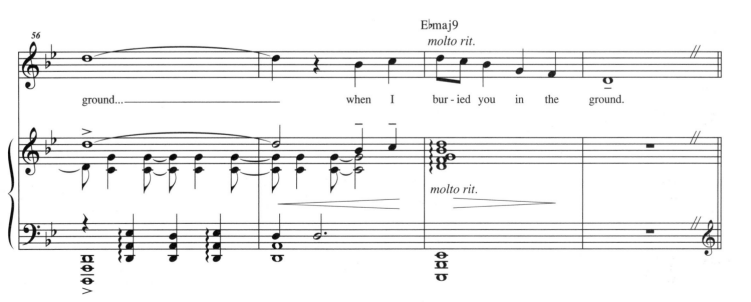

Tempo Primo